I0408839

Editor-in-Chief and Founder:
Lyndon H. LaRouche, Jr.
Editorial Board: *Lyndon H. LaRouche, Jr. , Helga Zepp-LaRouche, Robert Ingraham, Tony Papert, Gerald Rose, Dennis Small, Jeffrey Steinberg, William Wertz*
Co-Editors: *Robert Ingraham, Tony Papert*
Managing Editor: *Nancy Spannaus*
Technology: *Marsha Freeman*
Books: *Katherine Notley*
Ebooks: *Richard Burden*
Graphics: *Alan Yue*
Photos: *Stuart Lewis*
Circulation Manager: *Stanley Ezrol*

INTELLIGENCE DIRECTORS
Counterintelligence: *Jeffrey Steinberg, Michele Steinberg*
Economics: *John Hoefle, Marcia Merry Baker, Paul Gallagher*
History: *Anton Chaitkin*
Ibero-America: *Dennis Small*
Russia and Eastern Europe: *Rachel Douglas*
United States: *Debra Freeman*

INTERNATIONAL BUREAUS
Bogotá: *Miriam Redondo*
Berlin: *Rainer Apel*
Copenhagen: *Tom Gillesberg*
Houston: *Harley Schlanger*
Lima: *Sara Madueño*
Melbourne: *Robert Barwick*
Mexico City: *Gerardo Castilleja Chávez*
New Delhi: *Ramtanu Maitra*
Paris: *Christine Bierre*
Stockholm: *Ulf Sandmark*
United Nations, N.Y.C.: *Leni Rubinstein*
Washington, D.C.: *William Jones*
Wiesbaden: *Göran Haglund*

ON THE WEB
e-mail: eirns@larouchepub.com
www.larouchepub.com
www.executiveintelligencereview.com
www.larouchepub.com/eiw
Webmaster: *John Sigerson*
Assistant Webmaster: *George Hollis*
Editor, Arabic-language edition: *Hussein Askary*

EIR (ISSN 0273-6314) *is published weekly (50 issues), by EIR News Service, Inc., P.O. Box 17390, Washington, D.C. 20041-0390. (703) 777-9451 ext. 415*

European Headquarters: E.I.R. GmbH, Postfach Bahnstrasse 9a, D-65205, Wiesbaden, Germany
Tel: 49-611-73650
Homepage: http://www.eirna.com
e-mail: eirna@eirna.com
Director: Georg Neudecker

Montreal, Canada: 514-461-1557

Denmark: EIR - Danmark, Sankt Knuds Vej 11, basement left, DK-1903 Frederiksberg, Denmark.
Tel.: +45 35 43 60 40, Fax: +45 35 43 87 57. e-mail: eirdk@hotmail.com.

Mexico City: EIR, Sor Juana Inés de la Cruz 242-2 Col. Agricultura C.P. 11360
Delegación M. Hidalgo, México D.F.
Tel. (5525) 5318-2301
eirmexico@gmail.com

Canada Post Publication Sales Agreement #40683579

Postmaster: Send all address changes to *EIR*, P.O. Box 17390, Washington, D.C. 20041-0390.

Signed articles in *EIR* represent the views of the authors, and not necessarily those of the Editorial Board.

America's Mission

EDITORIAL

HELGA ZEPP-LAROUCHE

The Foreign Power Corrupting U.S. Politics Is London, not Moscow

Helga Zepp-LaRouche is the chairwoman of the German political party Civil Rights Movement Solidarity (BüSo)

Jan. 13—The unprecedented hysteria of the mainstream media and the neocons on both sides of the Atlantic over the election of Donald Trump is material for a first-class object lesson on the real dynamic now unfolding on the global strategic stage. It makes crystal clear, even for the most naïve adherent of political correctness, that what is happening has nothing to do with the interests of one party, or one state, against another. It has to do with the methods used by a collapsing empire against the emergence of a new paradigm, the precise content of which has not yet been clearly defined, but which nonetheless represents the rejection of the system of globalization.

Precisely on the eve of Trump's first press conference as President-elect, the U.S. television network CNN, and Buzzfeed, an Internet media company, created a huge sensation by breaking the story of a 35-page dossier which, in addition to reporting unspeakable anecdotes about Trump's alleged sexual habits, claimed that there is evidence that Trump is a *de facto* a Russian agent. After the campaign—long since re-

New York Daily News/you tube
Christopher Steele

cc/Chatham House
Sir Andrew Wood

futed by cyber-experts—that Russia had hacked emails of the Democratic National Committee, systematically smeared Hillary Clinton, and thereby helped Trump get elected, this new action was intended to lay the groundwork—even before Trump occupies the White House—for a rapid impeachment.

The author of the dossier is Christopher Steele, a Russian expert from MI6, the British foreign intelligence service, who concocted the dossier in the summer of 2016. It circulated for months in U.S. media circles and was considered so dubious that no one was willing to publish it during the hot phase of the election campaign. It was given directly to FBI Director James Comey, and given to the FBI again by Senator John McCain, after he heard former British ambassador to Moscow Sir Andrew Wood praise Steele and his "integrity" on the sidelines of a security conference in Canada.

After the surge of propaganda about the Russians stealing the U.S. election, and after Trump's declaration that he found Julian Assange of Wikileaks more credible than the U.S. intelligence services, the three U.S. intelligence chiefs—Director of National Intelligence James Clapper, CIA Director John Brennan, and FBI

Director James Comey—briefed the U.S. Senate, as well as President Obama and President-elect Trump, on their version of the story. The 35-page dossier would have played no role, because it was not credible, had these three intelligence chiefs not appended a two-page summary of it to their documents. The dodgy dossier was thus given the status of serious intelligence information, and that was apparently the green light for CNN, Buzzfeed, and then the rest of the media to publish the whole 35-page dossier.

Eric Denécé

A day later Clapper telephoned Trump to stress, after the fact, that U.S. intelligence services were not the source of the dossier, and that he could not vouch for its accuracy or inaccuracy. In a highly unusual move, he then published a written declaration to this effect. Thus, after the three intelligence chiefs themselves had triggered the escalation, Clapper carried out a maneuver known in these circles as a CYA operation (cover your ass)—which in more polite German means they came up with a "diplomatic excuse."

Whose World Is Disintegrating?

What then is the issue here? Eric Denécé, director of the French Center for Intelligence Research, an independent think tank, published the following analysis under the heading, "A Shocking Lack of Proof," after he had read the report by the Department of Homeland Security and the FBI on the alleged Russian intervention into the U.S. election campaign:

The Washington Establishment was taken totally by surprise by Trump's victory and understood that a "great cleanup" would occur, in which many of its members would lose their political positions and economic spinoffs connected to their international alliances.[1]

This assessment is accurate, but characterizes only one aspect of the situation. Apparently the trans-Atlantic neoliberal establishment is having a very hard time accepting the fact that Trump was democratically

elected. Their "world is coming apart," as German Chancellor Angela Merkel put it; they are "very shocked," as her Defense Minister Ursula von der Leyen expressed it. The world that is coming apart is the unipolar world which the neocons of the Bush Administration put into effect when the Soviet Union broke up. At that point the neocons proclaimed the "Project for a New American Century" to consolidate a world empire on the basis of the Anglo-American special relationship.

Governments that would not buckle under to this unipolar world would be eliminated over the course of time through a policy of regime change—for example, by color revolutions financed from the outside, as Victoria Nuland unblushingly admitted in the case of Ukraine. The U.S. State Department alone spent $5 million there on NGOs. But this policy also involved direct military intervention under the pretext of the defense of democracy and human rights, as in such cases as Iraq, Libya, and Syria. And naturally, Russia and China were the ultimate targets of this regime change policy.

The European Union bureaucracy was the unnamed junior partner in this arrangement, a beneficiary of the globalization system and itself eager for maximal imperial expansion, as British diplomat Robert Cooper openly admitted,[2] and only sporadically entering into competition with the dominance of the City of London and Wall Street.

A prerequisite for membership in the unipolar world's Establishment Club was naturally the adoption of the official "narrative" that all these destabilizations of democratically elected governments and all of these wars were about "freedom," "democracy," and "human rights," while those targeted were always "dictators" and demons. And of course, all those who wore such unipolar glasses, when addressing the reasons refugees were fleeing, could not get beyond just repeating the term, because otherwise they would have had to con-

---

1. http://www.larouchepub.com/pr/2017/170109_lack_of_proof.html

2. Robert Cooper, "The Post-Modern State and the World Order" (2002) was reprinted in full in the *Guardian* under the headline, "The New Liberal Imperialism": https://www.theguardian.com/world/2002/apr/07/1

demn the illegitimate wars that have cost the lives of millions of people, and then they would have been thrown out of the Club.

And now, with Trump, a person has won the U.S. election who, as Obama said of Putin, does not belong to "the team"; who agrees with Congresswoman Tulsi Gabbard and an array of conservative military figures that these regime-change wars must be stopped; and who even, as the ultimate desecration of taboos, wants to re-establish normal relations with Russia!

Respected U.S. investigative reporter Robert Parry compared the methods being used by the American intelligence services against Trump to J. Edgar Hoover's blackmail tactics. But the crude methods of Christopher Steele are also reminiscent of the "Troopergate" scandal against President Bill Clinton in the early days of his presidency, also inspired by British intelligence, which attempted, with a certain amount of success, to present Clinton as an unrestrained sex addict. This set the stage, so to speak, for the later Lewinsky affair, also launched by British intelligence, which aimed at destroying Clinton's presidency.

Out in the Open

What is spectacular about the operation against Trump, however, is that British intelligence and its American counterparts, which have operated for decades as spooks in the shadows, have now been forced to expose themselves openly. The essentially dilettantish operation—conducted by Steele, the man in charge of exposing the corruption in Fifa and the principal MI6

Russia Insider/you tube

Robert Parry

agent in the affair of Litvinenko's murder—revealed the direct intervention of the British Empire, for which the term "globalization" is only a synonym, into the internal affairs of the United States.

This empire is something other than the nations of the United States and Great Britain. It is the oligarchical forces exerting their power through the trans-Atlantic neoliberal financial system and the military defense of the unipolar world order, and they don't care a whit about the general welfare of the populations in whose nations they happen to live. A global revolution is underway against this empire, which found expression in the Brexit, just as it did in Trump's victory and the "no" to Renzi's referendum in Italy.

The assertion that Putin stole the election from Hillary Clinton, or that he will meddle in the coming elections in several European countries, is the collapsing empire's desperate attempt to somehow hold on to the authority to control the narrative.

Meanwhile, the new paradigm is developing in the form of a new world economic order, in which the BRICS countries and China's New Silk Road policy are offering win-win cooperation to all of the world's nations, in which all can only gain through the benefit of all—each through "the advantage of the other." If Trump succeeds in working with this new combination—which will only become clear after he is in office—it could mean a new era for mankind, in which sovereign nations work together for the future of mankind as a community of common destiny, and the era of empires is finally buried.

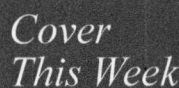Contents

www.larouchepub.com Volume 44, Number 3, January 20, 2017

Cover This Week

President John F. Kennedy, Rev. Martin Luther King, Jr. and Lyndon H. LaRouche, Jr.

I. The Great Change Under Way

Donald Trump and the New International Paradigm

Helga Zepp-LaRouche at the Stockholm EIR/Schiller Institute Seminar, Jan. 11, 2017 (edited presentation) https://youtu.be/cdl0Hxg_Ubc

"Sublime" is the only fitting word to describe Helga Zepp-La-Rouche's deep and beautiful presentation and the atmosphere she created in the audience of 60 participants (full room capacity) at the Schiller Institute/EIR seminar held in Stockholm on January 11th, under the title "Donald Trump and the New International Paradigm." Her speech moved the audience to address the fundamental epistemological, deeper meaning of the New Silk Road, and the meaning of the development of mankind in the universe. This deeper meaning even touched the diplomats present. An ambassador from an important Asian country started to discuss exactly the need to address these broader cultural and human implications, during the question period.

In all, there were seventeen diplomats present, among them seven ambassadors. Four European countries were represented, nine from Asia, and four from Africa. Among the other participants, there were contacts from different Swedish associations working for friendship with Russia, Ukraine, Syria, Yemen, Somalia, and the Baltic Sea area, and another group working to leave the EU.

The Chairman of the Schiller Institute in Sweden, Hussein Askary, moderated, and welcomed the participants. Helga Zepp-LaRouche then gave the keynote

EIRNS

Hussein Askary

address, in which she evaluated the ongoing struggle to turn around the election of Donald Trump by the outgoing neoconservatives and mainstream media. She pointed to the broad reaction to the neoliberal-instigated disaster as the real basis for the election of Trump, as well as other such reactions around the world, and said that is the place to look for the reason why Trump was elected, and not any hacking of computers. As the audience members were mainly new people, she presented the history of the Schiller Institute, which is also the history of the New Silk Road policy. She described how the economy evolves from one platform to another, and pointed to the Chinese policy for pushing for the next platform of the economy with Moon-based industrial development, for the further development of mankind as a non-Earth-bound species. The Chinese motivations for their worldwide policy came up in the discussion period, in the context of Africa. Helga then stressed, with her background of long study of China's history and Confucian thought, that her conclusion is that China is really pursuing a "win-win" policy based on the Confucian notion of pursuit of wisdom and harmony. She stressed the need for a Classical renaissance for the New Paradigm to succeed, and that this is something we cannot leave to Trump.

Helga Zepp-LaRouche: Good day, ladies and gentlemen. We are indeed in very, very fascinating times. And I think there is much reason to be hopeful. I know that for the last sixteen years, most people in the United States and Europe thought there is no great future. But I think that there are accumulations of strategic realignments which have shaped up over the last three years, but especially in the last year, where one can actually see that the potential for a completely new kind of relation among nations is on the horizon, and that we may actually have the chance to bring a peaceful world.

Now, obviously, in the system of globalization as we have known it, especially since the collapse of the Soviet Union, that system is completely unhinged and this is cause for a lot of freaked-out reactions by those people who were the beneficiaries of that system of globalization, but I will hopefully be able to develop that this is a temporary phenomenon, and it will be replaced by some more optimistic developments.

What we see right now is a completely new paradigm emerging, a system which is based on the development of all, a "win-win" potential to cooperate among nations, and obviously the idea for what was the axiomatic basis of the globalization system since 1991 to insist on a unipolar world, is failing, or has failed already. And with that, a system which tried to maintain this unipolar world with the policy of regime change, of color revolution, or humanitarian intervention, or so-called humanitarian intervention to defend democracy and human rights, obviously has led the world to a terrible condition, but this is now coming to an end.

So obviously, the statement by Francis Fukuyama at the end of the Soviet Union that this was the "end of history" and that there would be now only democracy, was really premature; because you have a complete backlash right now, which takes different forms in different in different parts of the world against this system of glo-

Helga Zepp-LaRouche at the Stockholm event.

EIRNS

balization, and in the Asian countries it takes the form of more and more countries joining with the New Silk Road perspective offered by China, the offer to work together in a "win-win" cooperation with the Belt and Road Initiative which is now already involving more than 100 nations and international organizations; and is already engaged in the largest infrastructure project in the history of mankind.

This new paradigm economic system already involves 4.4 billion people; it is already, in terms of spending, in terms of buying power in today's dollars, twelve times as big as the Marshall Plan was after the Second World War, and is open for every country to join, including Sweden, including the United States, and including every other country on the planet. And I will talk about that in a little while.

And in the trans-Atlantic sector you have a different kind of anti-globalization revolt, which is still ongoing; it's not yet settled how this will turn out. It started in a visible form with the vote of the British population in June last year for the Brexit, which was the first real upset; everybody was taken totally unawares, except a few insiders. This anti-globalization revolt was obviously continued with the election of President Donald Trump in the United States; it was continued with the "no" to the Italian referendum organized by Prime Minister Matteo Renzi, to change the Constitution. And what's common to all of these developments, Brexit, Trump, the "no" to the referendum in Italy, is they are caused by a fundamental feeling of injustice of ever-larger parts of the population which were victims of that system, which increasingly made the rich richer, made more billionaires richer, but destroyed increasingly the middle range of society, and made the poor poorer. It is my deepest conviction that that revolt will continue until the causes of this injustice are removed, and it will continue—it will hold the measuring rod to President Trump, whether he will fulfill his election promises;

and if he does not do that, I believe the same people would turn against Trump as they turned against Hillary.

What Is the Future of the Euro?

So that means that the future of the European Union and the euro is very doubtful. We have elections coming this year in France in April. This election, as of now, is completely up in the air. There is no firm prediction possible. You have a very tumultuous situation in Italy, where a coup was just attempted by Beppe Grillo and Verhofstadt in the European Parliament, which failed. They were trying to get the Five Star Party into the liberal group ALDE in the European Parliament, which was rejected by the liberal group, so it failed. Then you will have elections in Holland, and in September in Germany, where the star of Mrs. Merkel is also no longer as shiny as it may have been a while ago.

So we are looking at dramatic changes.

Now, let me start with the Trump election. In my whole political life, which is now becoming quite long, several decades—I have never in my whole political life, seen such hysteria on the side of the neocons, on the side of the mainstream politicians, and on the side of the liberal media, as concerning Trump. Now, admittedly, Trump does not fulfill the behavior code of Baron von Knigge, who was a German in the 18th century who developed the code for good diplomatic behavior. But what caused Trump's victory, is that he simply promised to end the political paradigm which was the basis of eight years of George W. Bush and eight years of Barack Obama, which was a direct continuation of the Bush-Cheney policy.

And it was a good thing, because it was very clear that if Hillary Clinton had won the election in the United States, that all the policies she was pursuing—including a no-fly zone over Syria, and an extremely bellicose policy towards Russia and China—would have meant that we would have been on the direct course to World War III. If you have any doubts about that I'm perfectly happy to answer questions about that, in the question and answer period.

So the fact that Hillary did not win the election was extremely important for the maintenance of world peace. And I think that of all the promises that Trump made so far, the fact that he said that he will normalize the relationship between the United States and Russia, is, in my view the most important step. Because if the relationship between the United States and Russia is

decent, and is based on trust and cooperation, I think there is a basis to solve all other problems in the world. And if that relationship were adversarial, world peace would be in extreme danger.

So from my standpoint, there is reason to believe that this will happen. The Russian reaction has been very moderate, but optimistic that this may happen. If you look at the appointments, you have several cabinet members and other people in high posts who are also for improving the relationship with Russia, such as Tillerson who is supposed to become Secretary of State, and General Flynn, who is a conservative military man but also for normalization with Russia, and many others, so I think this is a good sign.

Now, if you look at the reaction of the neocon/neoliberal faction on both sides of the Atlantic to this election of Trump, you can only describe it as completely hysterical. The *Washington Post* today has an article, "How To Remove Trump from Office," calling him a liar, just about every derogatory term you can possibly imagine, just on and on: unbelievable! The reaction in Germany was—von der Leyen, the Defense Minister, on the morning after the election said she was "deeply shocked," this was "terrible," this was a catastrophe, and it keeps going like that. So they have not recovered. And then naturally, you have the reports by the different U.S. intelligence services, Clapper, Brennan, Comey from the FBI—they all put out the claim that that it was Russian hacking of the emails of the DNC and Podesta which stole the election, because they allegedly shifted the view of the Americans to vote for Trump.

Now, I think this is ridiculous. Not only have many cyber experts, in Europe but also in the United States, already said that all the signs are that it was not a hacking but an insider leak got this information out. This is more and more likely, and there's absolutely zero proof that it was Russian hacking. Naturally, what is being covered up with this story, is what was the "hacking" about? It was "hacking" of emails that proved that Hillary Clinton manipulated the election against Bernie Sanders! That is not being talked about any more; but I would say, look there, and there are many people who recognize it. For example, a very important French intelligence person, Eric Denécé, who is a top-level think tanker in France, said: Well, it is quite clear why they put out this story, because the neocons had to expect the great cleanup, and many of them would lose their positions, and this is why they all agreed on this story and changed the narrative.

Wikimedia Commons

Barack Obama and George W. Bush.

Neoliberal Injustice

The real narrative is that it was the injustice of the neoliberal system of globalization which simply violated the interests of the majority of the people, especially in the "Rust Belt." Hillary Clinton in the election campaign was so arrogant that she didn't even go to Ohio or some of the other states which were formerly industrialized, where you have to see that the United States—contrary to what mostly is reported in the Western media in Europe—the United States is in a state of economic collapse. It has for the first time a falling life-expectancy; there is one indicator which shows whether a society is doing well or badly, and that is whether the life-expectancy increases or falls. In the United States it's falling for the first time for both men and women. In the period of the sixteen years of Bush-Cheney and Obama, which you can take as one package, the suicide rate has quadrupled in all age brackets; the reasons being alcoholism, drug addiction, hopelessness, and depression because of unemployment. There are about 94 million Americans who are of working age who are not even counted in the statistics, because they have given up all hope of ever finding a job again. If you have recently travelled in the United States, the United States is really in a terrible condition; the infrastructure is in a horrible condition, and people are just not happy.

So the vote, therefore, the narrative—that was the reason why Hillary was voted out, because she was per-ceived as the direct continuation of these sixteen years, and so the attempt to change that narrative by saying it was "Russian hacking" is pretty obvious.

Now, however, we have nine days left, until the new President comes in. And this is not a period of relaxation, because again, in an unprecedented way, the old team of Obama is trying to create conditions for the incoming President Trump to force him to continue on the pathway of Obama. For example, just a couple of days ago, they started a deployment of U.S. and NATO troops to the Russian border in the Baltics, in Poland, and in Romania, through the German city of Bremerhaven, where 6,000 troops landed with heavy military equipment; for example: U.S. Abrams tanks, Paladin artillery, Bradley fighting vehicles, 2,800 pieces of military hardware, 50 Black Hawk helicopters. This involving 1,800 personnel, with 400 troops to be attached to the 24 Apache helicopters.

Now, obviously, the deployment of this is supposed to be a provocation against Russia, and it's supposed to make it very difficult for Trump to start to improve relations.

A second area where you can see this effort to pin Trump down, is the question of the THAAD missiles in Korea, where now North Korea has claimed to be able to be able to launch their ICBMs anywhere, any time; and according to Chinese experts, the United States is entirely to blame for the fact that North Korea is behaving this way.

In South Korea, outgoing President Park Geun-hye, who may be impeached soon—actually in days or weeks—has agreed to accept a special task force of 1,000-2,000 which is supposed to eliminate the Pyongyang command under conditions of war, including Kim Jong-un; and obviously this is aggravating the situation, because given the history of such things, one is not sure when is the moment for such action.

Thirdly you can see it with the deployment of the U.S. aircraft carrier group USS Carl Vinson to the Western Pacific, in the vicinity of China. This aircraft carrier is of the nuclear-powered Nimitz class, and it will arrive exactly on 20th of January, the day Trump takes office. *Global Times*, the official Chinese newspaper, said that this deployment is set to disrupt potential talks between China and other countries in the region; naturally, it's also supposed to put a sour note into U.S.-China relations.

There are other efforts to change and determine the narrative in the post-Obama period. Ash Carter, the U.S. Secretary of Defense, just gave a press conference where he said that it was only the United States which has fought ISIS in Syria. Now, it takes some nerve to say that, because everybody in the whole world knows that without President Putin's decision to militarily intervene in Syria starting in September 2015, and the tremendous support of the Russian Aerospace Forces for the fighting of the Syrian troops, the present military situation in Syria would have never developed. And it was to the contrary, the very dubious behavior of the United States supporting various kinds of terrorist groups which prolonged this process and slowed it down.

But also in the attempt to pin down the narrative, it was John Kerry who, a week or so ago, gave a speech saying that it was the British Parliament which prevented a U.S. military intervention in Syria. Now—I mean, all of these people must think that the whole world has a very short memory, because I remember very vividly that it was Gen. Michael Flynn, in his capacity as head of the DIA [Defense Intelligence Agency], who had put out a public statement that it was the intention of the Obama administration to build up a caliphate in the region, in order to have regime-change against Assad, and he was then fired by [DNI] Clapper. And it is of a certain irony that, just last Friday, when Trump met with Clapper, Brennan and Comey in Trump Tower, where these three gentlemen wanted to impress Trump with their story about the Russian hacking,—the other person who was with Trump was General Flynn, who is now in the driver's seat as the incoming National Security Advisor. In any case, you can expect the truth not be suppressed forever. And as a matter of fact, it was in the moment shortly before the U.S. military intervention in 2013, when the U.S. military action was prepared to occur Sunday evening; we had gotten that from well-informed circles in Washington,—and then at the very last minute, the chairman of the Joint Chiefs of Staff, Gen. Martin Dempsey, went to Obama and said: "You should not start a war where you don't know how it ends. And if you don't ask the Congress, you will be impeached, or you run the risk of being impeached." And only because of that, did Obama go to ask the U.S. Congress. The U.S. Congress voted no, and the U.S. military intervention was prevented.

So this was quite different. And you know this attempt to fix the narrative will not be successful.

The Trump Administration

Now, I cannot tell you what this Trump administration is going to be. I think I mentioned the one point I'm pretty confident about: I think we will see probably only by February or even into March who will be actually in his cabinet, who will get approved by the Senate. But there are other interesting elements. For example: Trump had promised in the election campaign to invest $1 trillion into the renewal of the infrastructure in the United States. That is very good, as I said, because the United States urgently needs repair. It will, however, only function if at the same time, another promise by Trump, namely, what he promised in October in North Carolina, that he would implement the 21st Century Glass-Steagall Act, is also carried out, because the trans-Atlantic financial system remains on the verge of bankruptcy. You could have a repetition of the 2008 financial crash at any moment; and only if you have a Glass-Steagall law in the tradition of Franklin D. Roosevelt—what Roosevelt did in 1933 by separation of the banks, by getting rid of the criminal element of the banking system, and then replacing it by a credit policy in the tradition of Alexander Hamilton—can you remedy this situation. Otherwise, you cannot finance $1 trillion in infrastructure.

But one step in a positive direction is the fact that for example the former deputy foreign minister of China, and chairwoman of the Foreign Affairs committee of the National People's Congress, Mme. Fu Ying, made a speech in New York, about six weeks ago, where she said that indeed the Trump infrastructure program can be a bridge to the New Silk Road program of China. And that is quite the case: Just yesterday, Trump met with Jack Ma, who is the chief executive of Alibaba, a Chinese e-commerce firm, and Jack Ma said that he can help Trump to create a million jobs in the United States by initiating a platform for U.S. small businessmen to sell to Chinese consumers over the next five years, and vice versa, how the Chinese can invest in the United States. Trump afterwards said this was a great meeting, we will do great things together; and Jack Ma said that Trump was a very smart man and they got along very well.

So this is very good, because the Schiller Institute in 2015 published a report calling for the United States to join the New Silk Road, which is a whole approach including how you have to have a fast train system for the

United States. As you know, China has built 20,000 km of high-speed train systems. This high-speed network has doubled in only three years, and is expected to nearly double again by 2025, and reach 45,000 km in 2030. And the United States has none.

So the United States urgently needs a fast train system connecting the East Coast, the West Coast and the Midwest. Build some new science cities in the South, and get rid of the drought in the Southwest, California and the other states. So there are many, many things which urgently need to be done.

The Schiller Institute

Okay. Now, let me make a few remarks about the Schiller Institute, given the fact that many of you may not know much about us. And I want to underline the fact that we are not commentators on this whole question, but that we are responsible for many of the ideas which are now coming into effect.

The Schiller Institute was created by me in 1984. At that time we had the intermediate-range missile crisis, which brought the world to the verge of World War III; if you remember, we had the Pershing 2, and the Russians the SS-20, both on permanent alert, where there was a very short warning time, and the relationship between Europe and the United States was really in a terrible condition.

So I created the Schiller Institute with the idea that you needed an institute, a think-tank to put the relations among nations on a completely different basis. One of the most important aspects of the work was to work towards the establishment of a just, new world economic order, in the tradition of the Non-Aligned Movement. And there, my husband, in 1975, had proposed to replace the IMF with an International Development Bank, which would organize large credits for technology transfer from the industrialized countries to the developing sector, to overcome underdevelopment.

That proposal went into the Colombo Resolution of the Non-Aligned Movement in 1976 in Sri Lanka. So we had the idea that that policy had to come back on the agenda, that we had to create economic development in the southern hemisphere, so that every human being on this planet could have dignified potential for their lives, to develop all the potentialities embedded in them.

But from the beginning, we said that such a new world economic order can only function if it's combined with a Classical Renaissance—that we have to reject the popular culture associated with modern glo-balization, because it is depraved and degenerate. And that we had to go back to the revival, a Renaissance, of the best traditions of every culture, and have a dialogue among them. For example, in Germany, obviously you would emphasize the German Classical culture of Schiller, Beethoven, and all of Classical music; in China, you would emphasize Confucius; in India you would emphasize the Vedic writings, Tagore, and so forth. So you would go and revive in every country simply what they have contributed to universal history, and make that known.

Now, the present Chinese policy of "win-win cooperation," is exactly an echo of what we had proposed since 1984, to replace geopolitics with an approach for the common aims of mankind. In 1984, my husband, Mr. LaRouche, also uniquely predicted the collapse of the Soviet Union. He said if the Soviet Union stuck to its then-prevailing policies of the Ogarkov Plan, that it would collapse in five years. Now, there was nobody else who was saying the Soviet Union would collapse; it was completely unthinkable—but we observed the economic problems. And on Oct. 12, 1988, my husband and I held a press conference in Berlin, in the Bristol Kempinski Hotel, where we said that Germany will soon be unified—nobody believed that either at the time—and Germany should adopt the development of Poland as a model for the transformation of the Comecon through high technology.

Now, in 1989 therefore, when the Berlin Wall came down, we were the only ones who were not surprised. As a matter of fact, we immediately published a report, on how a unified Germany should develop Poland, and we called this program, the "Productive Triangle Paris-Berlin-Vienna," which is an area the size of Japan. It had the highest concentration of industry, and the idea was to build development corridors from that Productive Triangle to Poland, Warsaw, Kiev, and the Balkans, and transform the Comecon that way. It was before the D.D.R. [East Germany] collapsed; and if that had been picked up, maybe the Soviet Union and the Comecon would not have collapsed.

But because you had Bush, Thatcher and Mitterrand, they did not like this at all. So in 1991, when the Soviet Union collapsed, we immediately proposed to expand this program of the Productive Triangle into the Eurasian Land-Bridge: The idea that you would connect the population and industrial centers of Europe with those of Asia, through development corridors. The Iron Curtain was no longer there, so it was the natural thing to have infrastructure corridors to develop the landlocked areas of Eurasia.

Now we proposed this at the time to all the countries of Eurasia, and the only country which responded positively was China. So in 1996, they organized a very big conference in Beijing, called "The Development of the Regions along the Eurasian Land-Bridge," and I was one of the speakers. And China at that point declared the development of the Eurasian Land-Bridge to be the long-term perspective of China through the year 2010.

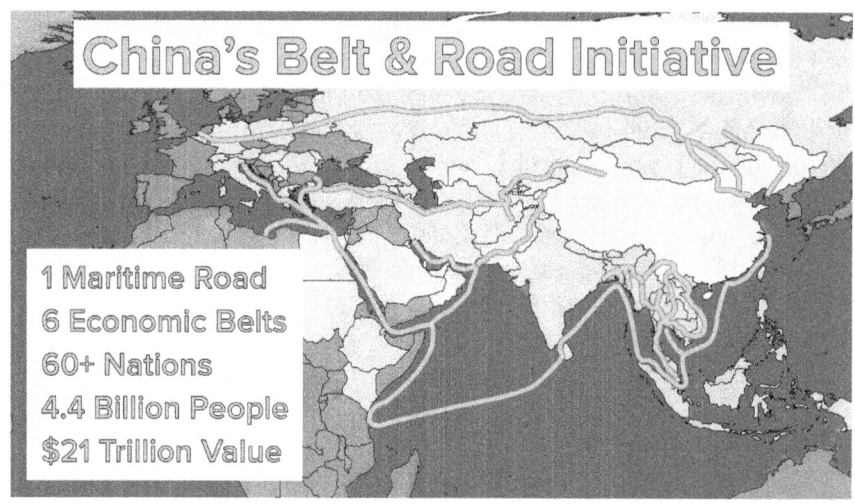

China's Belt & Road Initiative

1 Maritime Road
6 Economic Belts
60+ Nations
4.4 Billion People
$21 Trillion Value

EIRNS

As you know, then came the 1997-1998 Asia crisis and the Russian GKO crisis, so this whole development became interrupted. But that did not stop us from holding conferences about this proposal on five continents, in all U.S. cities, all European cities; and even in Latin America, in Sao Paolo and Rio; in New Delhi, and even in some African countries and Australia. We kept organizing for the idea that the natural next phase of the evolution of mankind would be the infrastructure connections of the entire planet.

Obviously, what also happened in 1999 was the repeal of the Glass-Steagall Act in the United States, which unleashed unregulated speculation, leading to the present bubble.

China Re-Adopts the New Silk Road

Now, in September 2013, when Xi Jinping in Kazakhstan announced the New Silk Road, we simply took all the different studies we had made during those twenty-four years, and published them, and we called it *The New Silk Road Becomes the World Land-Bridge*. This is a comprehensive proposal which has the yellow line there in the middle between China and Central Asia; this was the initial One Belt, One Road proposal by China, and we added simply—they also had the Maritime Silk Road—but we had a whole infrastructure program for Africa, for the South of Europe, the Balkans, with many corridors, including a Bering Strait Tunnel connecting the Eurasian infrastructure with the American system, with highways and high-speed trains all the way to Chile and Argentina. And eventually, when all of this is built, you will go by maglev train from the southern tip of South America to the Cape of Good Hope in Africa.

We published this proposal; and the actual book you can find at the book table, including an early report about this, from 1997. The first report we published in German, in 1991. This is not just about connection of infrastructure, but it has all the scientific conceptions of Mr. LaRouche's notion of physical economy.

Mr. LaRouche is probably the only economist in the West who deserves that name, because all the neo-liberal economists have been so wrong in their predictions that they should probably take another job. Mr. La-Rouche has given us his own scientific method, and in this report you will find such extremely important conceptions as the connection between energy-flux density in the production process, with the relative potential population density, which can be maintained with that energy-flux density, and there are other such important conceptions.

So this report was immediately published in China; the Chinese translated it into Chinese. We presented it in China in 2015. It was recommended by all the people who presented it, to all Chinese scholars, as the standard text on the Silk Road; and it has been sent to all major faculties and universities in China.

It was also published in Arabic, as you will hear from Hussein Askary. And it is now coming out shortly in Korean, in German, and we have requests for it to come out in other languages also.

So, while we were publishing these reports, the New Silk Road promoted by China has taken on a breathtaking dynamic. It has a few different names—first they called it "One Belt, One Road"; now they call it the "Belt and Road Initiative"; I always call it the "New Marshall Plan Silk Road," so that people get an idea.

New Development Corridors Spring Up

In the meantime, many of these proposals are in different phases of realization. There is the Maritime Silk Road, as you see on the maps. And China is building six overland economic corridors—as I said, it involves 70 nations, and over 30 international large organizations, 4.4 billion people, and trillions in investments. And as I said, already now it's 12 times bigger than the Marshall Plan was.

There is the original One Belt, One Road, connecting China and Central and West Asia through an economic corridor. In June 2015, China and the five Central Asian governments agreed to build that, and additional routes are being planned to go into Afghanistan. One is already going into Iran; when President Xi was in Iran last year, he promised—or they both promised—that they would extend this New Silk Road beyond Iran into Iraq, Afghanistan, Syria, Turkey.

There is the new Eurasian Land-Bridge which connects China with Western Europe, and it has already shortened the transport time for cargo, to two to three weeks from China, to different cities—from Chengdu, Chongqing, and Yiwu, to Duisburg, Lyon, Rotterdam, and Hamburg, from five weeks via ocean. Already by mid-2016, there were over 2,000 rail shipments from China to Europe, and it is picking up speed. All the cities in Europe that are termini, such as Madrid, Lyon, Duisburg, they're all happy; they realize that they have tremendous benefits from it.

There is the China-Mongolia-Russia corridor. In June 2016, the three presidents signed a trilateral economic partnership, at the 11th Shanghai Cooperation Organization meeting; and this corridor alone involves 32 projects.

There is the China-Pakistan economic corridor, which is creating 700,000 new jobs in Pakistan. It will produce 10,400 MW of power capacity, and the investment of $46 billion by the Chinese in this corridor equals all the foreign investment since 1970 in Pakistan.

There is the China-Myanmar-Bangladesh corridor.

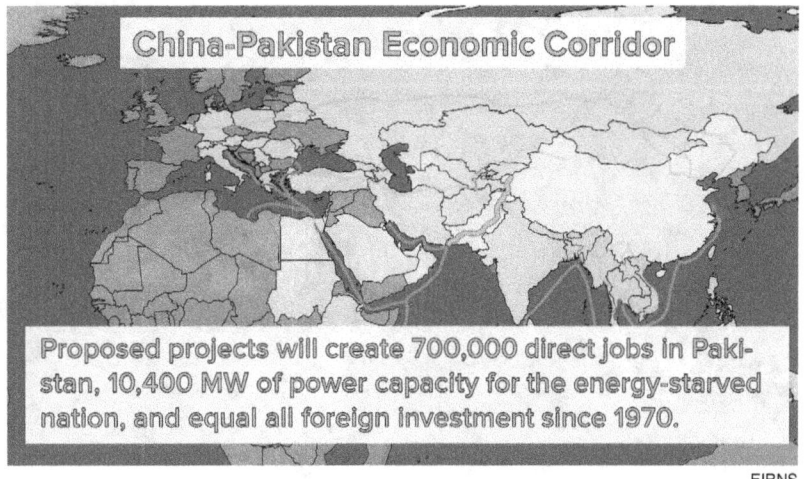

China-Pakistan Economic Corridor

Proposed projects will create 700,000 direct jobs in Pakistan, 10,400 MW of power capacity for the energy-starved nation, and equal all foreign investment since 1970.

EIRNS

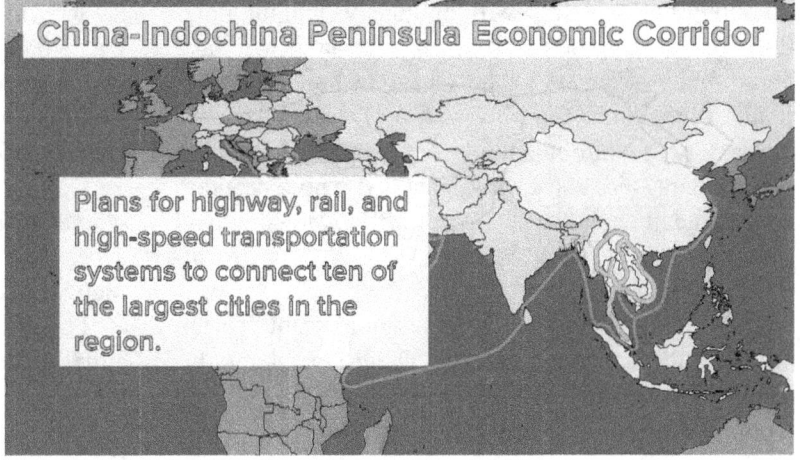

China-Indochina Peninsula Economic Corridor

Plans for highway, rail, and high-speed transportation systems to connect ten of the largest cities in the region.

EIRNS

This is creating an express highway between India and China for the first time, and it goes through Bangladesh and Myanmar. This corridor will be 1.65 million square kilometers; it will encompass 440 million people.

There is the China-Indochina Peninsula corridor. This will be a highway/rail and high-speed transport system connecting the ten largest cities of the region.

In Africa, we have the Djibouti-Ethiopia route. Because, as we know, Europe has been in large part destabilized by the refugee crisis, and there is a very big incentive, one would think, for Europeans to help develop Africa. But so far it is not coming from Europe, it's coming from China, India and Japan.

So, the Djibouti-Ethiopia railway just opened yesterday, so this is extremely good news. It opened yesterday, from Djibouti to Addis Ababa, 750 km, and it was built by China; it employed about 20,000 Ethiopians and 5,000 Djiboutians, and it will be connected to the standard gauge railway in Kenya, which again, created

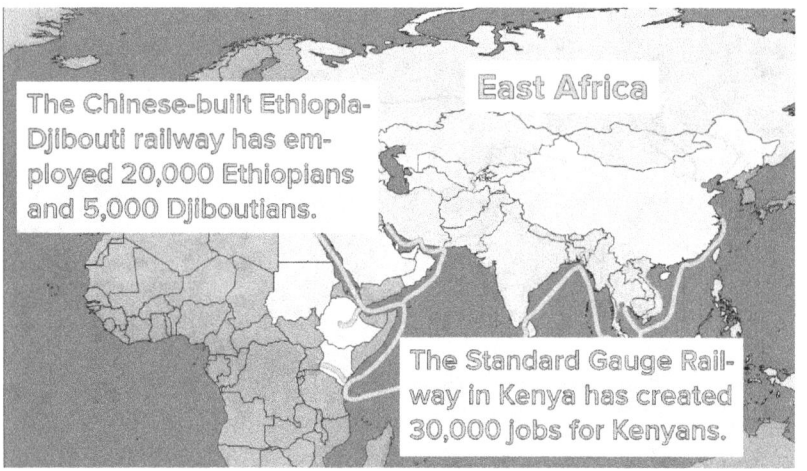

The Chinese-built Ethiopia-Djibouti railway has employed 20,000 Ethiopians and 5,000 Djiboutians.

The Standard Gauge Railway in Kenya has created 30,000 jobs for Kenyans.

EIRNS

30,000 jobs. And this will obviously, among other things, transform the port of Mombasa, and it will take cargo and passengers to the Ugandan border in one-tenth of the time it takes by road. A professor from the University of Nairobi School of Diplomacy, Prof. Gerishon Ikiara said, and I agree, that this whole program will "radically transform African participation in global trade in the next two decades and will catalyze the industrial transformation of Africa."

Now, there is another extremely important project, which is the Transaqua project. There is a Memorandum of Understanding between the Lake Chad Basin Commission and the Chinese engineering firm PowerChina. Now PowerChina is the company which built the Three Gorges Dam and several other large projects, so they really know what they're doing; and they agreed in this contract to do a feasibility study for the Transaqua project.

This is the largest infrastructure project ever entertained in Africa. It was developed in the late 1970s by the Italian firm Bonifica, and there, in particular, by Dr. Marcello Vichi. Mr. LaRouche has promoted this project since he got news of it, because it was a perfect way of solving many problems at the same time. As you know, Lake Chad is shrinking; it is presently only about less than 10% of its original size, and it affects the life of the entire people, 40 million people, in the Chad Basin. And naturally, it is already having drought effects and so forth.

The concept is simply to transfer water from the Congo River, using the unused discharge of the Congo River water going into the ocean. Now, the Congo River is the second largest river in the world, and it discharges 41,000 cubic meters/second into the ocean—unused.

And the idea is to take only 3-4% of that water and bring it into Lake Chad. There was a big campaign trying to convince the people in the different states along the Congo River that it's stealing their water, and so forth, but that was really an effort by the Greenies, and it has no substance to it whatsoever.

First of all, the idea is not to take the water from the Congo River, but from the west bank tributaries at an altitude that allows one to bring water by gravity into the Chad/Central African Republic watershed, which is at an elevation of 500 meters, and then pour it into the Chari River, which is a tributary of Lake Chad. So this way you would create a 2,400 km long waterway which would eventually bring 100 billion cubic meters of water per year into Lake Chad, and also create navigable infrastructure.

Obviously, the Democratic Republic of Congo would be also a big beneficiary, because it would obtain access to a navigable waterway, electricity production, regulation of rivers and so forth.

PowerChina is now financing a feasibility study for a first phase of the project which would involve building a series of dams in the Democratic Republic of Congo, the Republic of Congo, and the Central African Republic. It would also potentially generate 15-25 billion kilowatt-hours of hydroelectricity through the mass movement of water by gravity; it would potentially create a series of irrigated areas for crops and livestock, of an area of 50-70,000 sq km in the Sahel zone in Chad, in the northeast of Nigeria, in the north of Cameroon, and in Niger. It would also make possible an expanded economic zone, creating a new economic platform for agriculture, industry, transportation, and electricity for twelve African nations.

So PowerChina has put up $1.8 million for the first phase of the feasibility study, and if the construction starts, this is a big project, so it's not expected to be finished overnight, but it will take generations: But it will create livelihoods for 40 million people in the basin. And this is just one project, but there are many others. For example, Chinese Foreign Minister Wang Yi is just on a five-nation tour through Africa, and was already in Madagascar and Tanzania, and is going to Zambia, Nigeria, and Republic of Congo, and he's inviting all African nations to join the Belt and Road Initiative.

We have proposed an expanded program of railways and nuclear power, just transforming the entire African continent.

In Latin America

There are development plans for Latin America, high-speed railway routes in Latin America, which the Schiller Institute has proposed. In 1982, when Mr. LaRouche was working with President Jose Lopez Portillo of Mexico on these projects, he called it "Operation Juarez," to refer back to the best traditions of Mexican-American cooperation. And these are all projects which are obvious. If you look at a map of Africa or Latin America, you don't see that kind of infrastructure! If you see some railway, you see it as a small line from a mine to the port to exploit the raw materials, but you don't have infrastructure. And we had this idea, which Alexander von Humboldt, by the way, proposed in 19th Century, so it's not that revolutionary; it's sort of obvious.

The Chinese have made various proposals since the BRICS summit in Brazil in July 2014. There is a northern route of the Brazil-Peru transcontinental rail line. This was already agreed upon between the governments of Brazil and China a year ago; but then they had the coup in Brazil, Dilma Rousseff was impeached, so this came to a halt; also the new government in Peru is very reluctant. But there's a big movement: I just addressed a conference of economists in the Amazon region two months ago, and there's a whole movement, also associated with the Fujimori party, who absolutely want to fight for that rail line because it is the step to the future.

There are three additional lines. One line would include Bolivia in this rail line, and there are three additional lines through Argentina and Chile; China also wants to build three tunnels between Chile and Argentina to connect the Pacific and the Atlantic.

This is the Nicaragua Canal, which is in the early stages of completion, also built by China. This will increase the speed of global shipping between Belem and Shanghai, and cut the time of the current route across the Atlantic and around Africa by 10%.

So I can only mention the most important projects. There are many, many others. For example, China and Ecuador are building a science city in Ecuador. President Correa, during the recent state visit of President Xi Jinping, said that the collaboration between Ecuador and China will mean that Ecuador soon will be on the same level as all industrialized countries. They have the idea of overcoming poverty forever. The science city is going to do work in the most advanced fields of science.

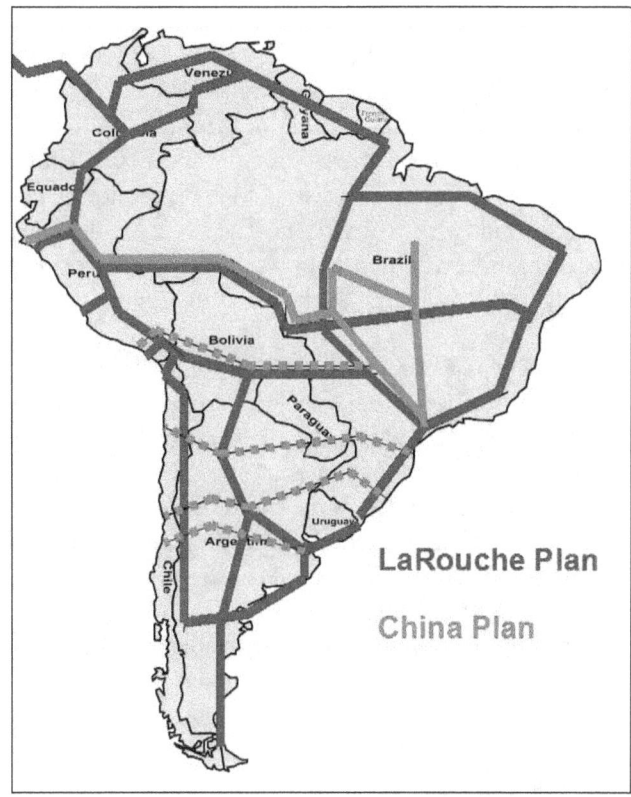

LaRouche Plan

China Plan

EIRNS

Bolivia, which used to be a coca producing country, is now cooperating on space projects with China, with Russia, with India. So there is a completely new mood!

A Completely New Mood

I talked with many Africans—there was a big conference in Hamburg just a couple of months ago, where the Africans said that there is a completely new mood in Africa, there is a new paradigm: China, Japan, India are all investing, and the Europeans, if they don't shape up, will become marginal and irrelevant. So there is a completely new optimism caused by this dynamic.

Now, just on the diplomatic level, this process of integration is going absolutely rapidly, especially since September of last year, when you had on Sept. 2-3, the Eastern Economic Forum in Vladivostok, where the integration of the Eurasian Economic Union and the Belt and Road Initiative was on the table. Japanese Prime Minister Shinzo Abe participated in that conference, and Japan is now massively investing in the Far East of Russia, in terms of energy cooperation. Putin was just in Japan, on a state visit; Abe will go on a state visit to Russia this year. They're talking about settling the conflict concerning the Northern Islands, the Kuril Islands. They're talking about a peace treaty between

Russia and Japan, and obviously there is a complete strategic realignment going on. President Duterte changed the role of the Philippines from being the aircraft carrier for the United States in the South China Sea, to now collaborating with China on economic cooperation, and also with Russia. The same, by the way, goes for Turkey, which is now shifting and working with Russia, Iran and Syria, to bring peace to the region.

So there is a complete strategic realignment going on, and the Western media and Western politicians have just not got it yet. But this is very, very interesting.

So then this momentum continued. From Vladivostok, immediately afterwards, on Sept. 4-5, to the G20 Summit in Hangzhou, where China took real leadership in saying the future recovery of the world economy must be based on innovation and Xi made very clear that this innovation must be shared with the developing countries, so as not to hold up or hinder their development.

So, it's a completely new paradigm, and I'll say something about that in a second.

Then you continue to the ASEAN meeting in Laos, the BRICS meeting in Goa, India, in October, the APEC meeting in Lima in November, and it involves all of these organizations and is spreading very fast.

Why doesn't Europe join this? Look, Europe is in bad shape. The EU is collapsing, the people in Italy by now hate the European Central Bank, they hate Merkel, they hate Schäuble, they hold Merkel responsible for the suffering of the population in Italy, which is now reaching dimensions like Greece; Greece was destroyed—one-third of the Greek economy was destroyed by the austerity policy of the Troika. And you know, there's nothing left of the idea of unity in Europe. There are borders being built, the Schengen policy is dead; look at the Eastern European countries—the Eastern European and Central European countries are reorienting towards China! The 16+1 are the Central and East European Countries; they have extensive infrastructure cooperation with China. China is building up Piraeus port in Greece; they're building a fast railway between Budapest and Belgrade, and many other projects.

The Problem in Europe

But the problem with Europe, is that at least the European EU bureaucracy and some governments, like the German government, are are still on the old paradigm, the geopolitical paradigm of globalization, of neoliberal policies, and they don't understand that by what China has proposed, and what is now the basis of a very close and determined strategic partnership between Russia and China—they have put on the agenda a different model: To overcome geopolitics by a "win-win" strategy. Now, most people, at least in Europe and in the United States, have a very hard time understanding that. They cannot imagine that governments are for the common good, because we have not experienced that for such a long time. The common idea of all the think-tanks, or most think-tanks, is "China must have ulterior motives"; "China is just trying to replace Anglo-American imperialism, with a Chinese imperialism." But that is not true! I mean, I'm not naive: I have studied this extensively. I was in China for the first time in 1971, in the middle of the Cultural Revolution. I have seen China as it was then, I travelled to Beijing, Tianjin, Qingdao, Shanghai, and to the countryside, and so I know what an enormous transformation China has made in this period.

I went back to China in 1996, after 25 years; already then it was breathtaking. But if you look, the Chinese economic model has raised 700 million people from extreme poverty to a decent living standard; China is now committed to developing the interior region as part of their building of the New Silk Road, to eliminate poverty from China totally by the year 2020—and there are only 4% left in poverty right now.

Now, China is offering their Chinese economic model to all participating countries in this New Silk Road conception, and it is in the interest of Sweden. It would be in the interest of Germany, because Germany is still—despite the Green insanity which has deformed many brains—is still a productive country. The German *Mittelstand* (small and medium industry) is still producing, I think, the third largest number of patents in the world. It is their natural interest to find cooperation not only in bilateral cooperation, but in investments in third countries. It would be in the best interest of Germany: if Germany is freaked out about the refugees, which really has meant a complete destabilization of the country, then why is Germany not cooperating with Russia, China, India, and Iran, in the reconstruction of the Middle East? Now the Syrian government has started to rebuild Aleppo, at least to rebuild the hospitals and the schools. The Schiller Institute proposed in 2012, a comprehensive proposal for the development of the entire Middle East, from Afghanistan to the Mediterranean, from the Caucasus to the Gulf States, and it would be in the absolute self-interest of Germany because—sure you have to destroy ISIS and the terrorists with military means—but then you have to create conditions where young people in Syria, Iraq, Afghanistan, and Yemen, have a reason to become doctors, scientists, and teachers, so that they have a future, in that way you drive out terrorism forever!

And if all the big neighbors would cooperate—Russia, China, India, Iran, Egypt, Turkey, Italy, France, Germany, and Sweden—you could change this region in no time! And you will hear about that soon from Hussein.

The same for Africa. The only minister in Germany who is reasonable is Development Minister Gerd Müller, because he travels all the time to Africa and he says there

NASA

Apollo 17 lunar roving vehicle.

will be the need for many millions of jobs for the young people of Africa in the next years; if we don't create these jobs, many, many millions of people will flee from hunger and war and epidemics.

So would it not be in their self-interest that all the European nations join hands with the Chinese Silk Road initiative, and help to reconstruct and build up the economies of Southwest Asia and Africa? I think that that mission would also really help to overcome the disunity of Europe, because you will not solve that problem by looking at your navel; but you will solve that problem by a joint mission for the greater good of mankind.

So, I think that this is all possible. It can happen this year, it can start this year, because China has committed itself to have two big summits this year—one summit will involve all the heads of state of the Belt and Road Initiative, and it can be the year of consolidation of the new paradigm.

Now there are a couple of elements which are also important for this new paradigm, because we are not just talking about infrastructure and overcoming poverty. The next phase of the evolution of man is not just to bring infrastructure to all continents on this planet, but to continue that infrastructure into nearby space around us. This was formulated in this way for the first

time by the great German-American space scientist and rocket scientist Krafft Ehricke, who made fundamental contributions to the Apollo project. He had the beautiful vision that if you look at the evolution over a longer period of time, life developed from the oceans with the help of photosynthesis; then you had the development of ever higher species, species with a higher metabolism, higher energy-flux density in their metabolism.

Eventually man arrived. Man first settled at the oceans and the rivers; then with the help of infrastructure, man developed the interior regions of the continents; and we are now with the World Land-Bridge picture—this will be, when it is built, the completion of that phase of the evolution of mankind, by simply bringing infrastructure into all the landlocked areas of the world, and with the help of new methods to create water, with modern technologies, we will create new, fresh water. For example, if you have peaceful nuclear energy, you can desalinate huge amounts of ocean water; through the ionization of moisture in the atmosphere, you can create new water to solve the problem of desertification. Right now all the deserts are growing; with these new technologies you can reverse that, make the deserts green, and just make this planet livable for all human beings!

But this is not the end: Mankind is not an Earth-bound species. Mankind is the only species which is capable of creative discovery, and the collaboration of all nations for space exploration and space research is the next phase of our evolution. Now China has a very ambitious space program. It landed the Yutu rover on the Moon in 2014. Next year it will go to the far side of the Moon, and eventually bring back helium-3 from the far side of the Moon, which will be an important fuel for fusion power economy on Earth. Right now, we are very close to making breakthroughs on fusion power. The Chinese EAST program [Experimental Advanced Superconducting Tokamak] has reached 50 million degrees in plasma for 60 seconds under high confinement. And just a couple of days ago, the plasma configuration in the stellarator in Greifswald, Germany, was proven accurate to one part in 100,000. But it means that in a few years, we can have fusion power! And that will create energy security, raw materials security, on Earth.

The Next Platforms for Civilization

We're looking at a completely new phase of civilization, and the far side of the Moon is very important because it will not have radio-frequency noise, as you have on the Earth-facing side of the Moon; this far side is shielded from a lot of this radio-frequency noise, so it will be possible to put up much better radio-telescopes, and so you will be able to look into Solar system, into the Galaxy, into other galaxies much, much farther than so far.

I don't know if any of you have seen the latest pictures from the Hubble telescope: If you have not done that, please, go home and take the time to look at these pictures from the Hubble telescope. I saw them, and I was completely excited, because now we know that there are—at least—two trillion galaxies! Now, I have a good imagination, but I cannot imagine that. It's just too big. And when you see the pictures which have already been taken, you have galaxies which look like the Milky Way; then you have totally different nebulas; you have all kinds of formations. And not one galaxy is like the other. Just imagine how big the Universe is!

And we know very, very little! But man is the only species which can know! No donkey will ever know about the great galaxies or—no dog will ever be able to breed rabbits to have a better breakfast. They all want a better breakfast, but they don't know how to do it. Man is capable of overcoming every limitation, and the mind

of man is a physical force in the Universe. We're not outside of the Universe, but what our mind invents or discovers, is part of the Universe. And that is a very exciting thing.

And there is lots to be found out about what is the origin and essence of life. What governs the laws of the Universe? What is the role of the mind in the Universe? I mean, these are all extremely exciting questions, and they all prove that man is not an Earth-bound species. So there is no need to be a Greenie, because we can apply man's knowledge to expand our role in the Universe. Even the European Space Agency is now talking about a "Village on the Moon."

Krafft Ehricke had said that building an industrial center on the Moon will be important as a stepping stone for further travel in space. And you now see the shaping up of new economic platforms. Mr. LaRouche has developed this notion of an economic platform to signify a period of economic development which is governed by certain laws, like for example, the development of the steam engine created a new platform; the development of the railway created a new platform; fission is creating a new platform. And the platform is always governed by the most advanced technologies of that time.

You can already see that in the infrastructural development of nearby space, the first platform is simply that man is able to reach Earth orbit! That's not self-evident. If you had told man in the Middle Ages that you will get on a spaceship and go into orbit, he would have said you're crazy!

Now we can already see we have manned space travel, and we can now connect to where the Apollo project stopped after the assassination of Kennedy, 40 years ago; but now China, India, Russia, they are all continuing that process. India also has an extremely ambitious space project.

And so, the first economic platform will be simply to leave the planet Earth and to go into orbit; the second economic platform of space research will be to have an industrial base on the Moon, and to eventually start to produce raw materials from space. Because you will, as this continues, not always transport materials from the Earth for your space travel, but once you have fusion as a propulsion fuel where the speed will become much greater, you will be able to take materials from asteroids and from other planets, for your production and your requirements in space. And then longer space travel between planets as the third platform, which is already visible.

This is very exciting, and once you start to think about it, it shows that mankind is really capable of magnificent achievements, and that we should really overcome geopolitics. Geopolitics is like a little, nasty two-year-old boy who is not yet educated, and who knows nothing better than to kick his brother in the knee. That's about the level of geopolitics. What Xi Jinping always talks about is that we have to form a "community of destiny for the common future of mankind," and that is exactly what the Schiller Institute set out to do in 1984, when we said we have to fight for the common aims of mankind. And these common aims of mankind must come first, and no nation should be allowed to have a national interest or the interest of a group of nations, if it violates these higher common aims of mankind. And the areas of working together include a crash program for fusion, space cooperation, and breakthroughs in fundamental science.

All of this however must be combined with a Classical Renaissance, a dialogue of cultures on the highest level, and we have already very successfully practiced that at Schiller Institute conferences, where we had European Classical music: Bach, Beethoven, Verdi, Schubert, and Schumann; Chinese Classical music;

Indian poetry. We will have this coming Saturday in New York, a beautiful event on dialogue of civilizations, of cultures, where we will have a Chinese professor talking about literati painting. You know, in Chinese painting, you have poetry, calligraphy and painting, in one. And for Westerners, it's a complete revelation, because this does not exist in European painting. People get completely excited, because they discover that there are beautiful things to discover in other cultures! And once you study and know these other cultures, xenophobia and racism disappear! Because you realize that it's beautiful that there are many cultures, because there are universal principles to be discovered in music. One musician will immediately understand another musician because it's a universal language. Scientists speak a universal language; they understand each other.

And so the future of civilization will be a dialogue between Plato, Schiller, Confucius, Tagore, and many other great poets and scientists of the past. So, if you give every child access to these things, which is also in reach, I can see that we will have a new era, a new civilization of mankind. And I would invite all of you to not just look at it, but be part of it.

Behind the Hoax About Russian Hacking

From an interview with Ray McGovern

The following article consists of excerpts from a lengthy interview with Ray McGovern. Mr. McGovern was a high-ranking CIA analyst from 1963 to 1990, and in the 1980s chaired National Intelligence Estimates and prepared the President's Daily Brief. In 2003, he co-founded Veteran Intelligence Professionals for Sanity. We at Executive Intelligence Review have the highest regard for Mr. McGovern and his ongoing efforts to get out the truth in regard to the current activities and functioning of the intelligence community and how this impacts U.S. policy making. At the same time, EIR is not in a position to make any final judgement as to the technical details of U.S. intelligence gathering.

LPAC

Ray McGovern

Jason Ross: It's January 10, 2017; I'm Jason Ross here at LaRouche PAC. We are very happy to have Ray McGovern in the studio today, multi-decade veteran of the CIA and the co-founder in 2003 of Veteran Intelligence Professionals for Sanity. Thanks very much for coming today, Ray.

Ray McGovern: You're most welcome; I'm glad to be with you.

Ross: So, let's jump right into one of the big issues that we're hearing about so much in the media today—the issue of purported Russian hacking of the U.S. elections. Now your group, the Veteran Intelligence Professionals for Sanity, released a press statement on December 12th, saying that all evidence pointed toward a leak rather than a hack. Since then, two reports have come out; one from the the the Department of Homeland Security (DHS) and one primarily authored by the ODNI, the Director of National Intelligence, saying here's the proof; we know Russia did it. The report was of questionable usefulness. Then just a few days ago, you co-authored an op-ed in the *Baltimore Sun* with William Binney, where you restated your position; all evidence points toward this being a leak rather than a hack, and in any case, evidence of a hack has not been presented. Why do you take that position?

McGovern: Well, I need to tell you something about Veteran Intelligence Professionals for Sanity first. We established ourselves when we saw that our colleagues—the colleagues with whom we had worked—had let themselves be suborned into creating, into fabricating intelligence for the express purpose of deceiving our elected representatives out of their Constitutional prerogatives to declare or otherwise authorize war. That was before Iraq; and that's as bad as it gets.

Bush, Cheney, and the others all said, "Oh, it was a terrible mistake." It was not a mistake; it was out and out fraud. When we saw that happening, we formed a little group—there were five of us in the beginning—and we started publishing. We published three memoranda before the war, warning the President. Our first one was on the day of Colin Powell's speech—the 5th of February, 2003—and we gave him a C-minus for content. And we warned the President, "The intelligence is being manipulated and you really should widen the circle of your advisors," we said at the end, "beyond those who are clearly bent on a war for which we see no compelling reason, and from which, we believe, the unintended consequences are likely to be catastrophic." We take no delight in the fact that we happened to be right on that; there were a couple of other people saying that, but nobody got into the mainstream media.

When this business about Russian hacking went viral, it was the most natural thing for me to say to my colleague Bill Binney, who had been the technical director at NSA before he left shortly after 9/11, "Hey, Bill. We need a memo from you; we need you to do a draft because you designed most of these systems, and you know what Ed Snowden has revealed. Those slides? They look really interesting to us, but we need somebody to take us through them." So, he said, "Sure." So, he gave us a draft, and what we typically do is, we circulate it around the five or six or seven people who have special interests in that, or special experience; and we got it right together. We were one of the first ones off the block saying "Yeah, this is a crock! Why? For technical reasons." There were plenty of other reasons, but some people—and I think it's to their credit—want to know, "Is this possible? Could the Russians have done this?" Well, the answer is "Yes, but NSA would know about it."

Now, it boggles the mind, Jason, it boggles the mind. But NSA traces *all emails on this planet*. If they (the emails) go abroad, they have cooperating agencies and cooperating governments. If they go through the United States, they get them; if they come from outside, they get them all. And they can trace them; they have these little trace mechanisms at various points in the network. So, they know where each and every email originates and where it ends up.

So, let's say the Russians hack, and they got it to Julian Assange, they got it to one of his associates. "Well, OK, Russians are really bad people," people say; "show us the messages." "Oh, we can't; we don't have the messages. But we'll look at it." Now, they got the President, before he went on vacation to Hawaii, to impose sanctions based on this elusive evidence that they can't show us. Now, add to that the ironclad coverage they have of the Ecuadoran embassy in London, where Julian is; and I'm sure that they monitor his colleagues as well, wherever they happen to be.

My first reaction was to laugh at them, but this a very sad thing to see what the intelligence community has become; very, very sad. Because this is an important issue.

So, what did the President do? He slapped on sanctions; threw out thirty-five diplomats. All on whose say-so? John Brennan's. Now, how did the *New York Times* get all this information? John Brennan. We know that because the *Wall Street Journal* was a little ticked off about it, and they said, "Yeah, it's Brennan that's talking to these other guys; he's not talking to the *Wall Street Journal*." So, what do we have here? We have the President going out on a limb, causing even more danger, more tensions, more flak in our relationship with Russia. On the basis of what? Well, let me just say this; maybe I'll put it this way: I was looking at some YouTube clips, and I happened on one of Christiane Amanpour, broadcasting from London. She's interviewing Lukyanov, one of the Russian gurus. She says, "Mr. Lukyanov, [imitating Amanpour's voice] you say there's zero evidence, you say zero. Well, if there's *zero* evidence, why is it that the President of the United States has slapped sanctions on Russia?"

Ross: Hah! That's good.

McGovern: [Earlier], I remember being asked that question about weapons of mass destruction. [Again imitating Amanpour's voice] "Mr. McGovern, if you say there's no evidence of weapons of mass destruction, why did Bush and Cheney start a war on Iraq?" Well, same answer; same answer! It's a really bad flashback, because what they need to do, is come up with the evidence. My strong view is that they're not going to do that; not because of sources and methods, but because there isn't any.

Ross: Because that's just not what happened.

McGovern: Well, one has to be careful in distinguishing these things. Do the Russians hack? Of course they hack! Chinese hackers—the Chinese got twenty million records from OPM, right? Everybody hacks. I'm sure the Russians have hacked; but the question is, who gave these records, these emails from the DNC—the Democratic National Committee—and from Podesta's email, to Julian Assange or his people to put out in that very overt form. Now Julian, of course, says it wasn't the Russians. John Brennan says it was the Russians. I like to believe government officials; I spent twenty-seven years in the CIA. I would really like to believe the Director of the CIA. But you know, experience with his record—and Clapper's record, Clapper having lied under oath to the Senate. And then after he was shown to have lied, he said, "Oh! What I said was clearly erroneous."—His words. And the Senate said, "Oh, tut, tut! Don't worry; no problem." That was four years ago; four *years* ago.

So, if you want to believe Clapper, you want to believe Brennan, that's your prerogative. I know Julian Assange; I had dinner with him right before the election, four days before the election. He looks awful. Stay inside for four years, plus; you look awful. He's got no color; he's pale. But he was enlivened; he had just done that interview with John Pilger. He was enlivened; and I know the feeling, because we're in the same business. We're trying to spread some truth around, OK? He had done that successfully. What he had, he ordered in a cogent way, made it eminently searchable; and when he put it out—and this is the real story—when he put out the DNC emails and the Hillary Clinton emails, he put them out very deliberately. He evinced this right before the Democrat National Convention—two days before. So, this caused quite a stir. What happened? Well, people forget, the first thing that happened, the top five officials—starting with that woman …

Ross: Debbie Wasserman Schultz.

McGovern: Debbie Wasserman Schultz. They quit! What does that tell you? The next thing, I can see them sitting around the table—the Brain Trust; and Hillary comes in and says, "How are we going to do this? Right before the convention! Anybody talking to Bernie?" Why did I say Bernie? These emails, the contents showed that she stole the nomination from Bernie Sanders; by every which way she did that.

Ross: Talk about an assault on democracy!

McGovern: Or interfering in the election! Yeah, it was interfering, but it was Hillary that did it. So, that's what they showed, OK? So, what do you do? Somebody says, "I know! We'll blame it on the Russians!" "But it wasn't the Russians, it was Julian Assange." "That's OK. He's probably working for the Russians; we'll say he's working for the Russians. There's a two-fer; we'll get the Russians, and we'll get Julian Assange, too." "That sounds great, but what's the rationale?" "Oh, c'mon! We'll say the Russians want Trump to win."

Sources and Methods

Ross: It seems bizarre sometimes to see the extent of the anti-Russia coverage in the media, from the administration... some of the recent coverage like the claim that Russia had hacked a Vermont power utility and was going to take over all of our power plants now. The evidence is not being put forward for this; it's covered up by saying we don't want to reveal our sources and methods, even when this is something that is being called by some senators "an act of war," when Obama is taking actions against Russia in response to it, increasing sanctions, you might think that this is the sort of time where it might be worth revealing what your sources and methods are, given the importance of the political changes it's provoking.

McGovern: I'm really glad you mention that, because I've been through this kind of thing. David Ignatius in the *Washington Post* today says, "our sources and methods"—they can't reveal their sources and methods, and the *New York Times* when they had that banner headline: "Putin Directed Attack...," even there, Scott Shane was sensible enough to say, "Well, there isn't any real evidence here and that's probably because of the sources and methods."

Ross: Right. Right.

McGovern: On the technical side, Bill Binney, as I said before, was the technical director at NSA, and he's open. He's very open in saying, "Look, what I know, I used to be unable to say. But when Ed Snowden came out with all these slides and all these diagrams, not only can I say 'Hey! Wow!' The systems that I put in place are still being used, but my God, they're not only being used abroad, they're being used in our country and this is how they do it." Ray, you see this? These are the trace mechanisms they put in the network. They're about 500 right here in Europe, and so he takes me through the whole thing. I said, "Well, is that secret?" He says, "Hellooo? No! The slides say 'Top Secret,' code word, but they're all revealed now. So, I can tell you Ray, and I can tell everybody that I'm 99 percent sure that if there are emails, if there are hacks, then we would have them." So is it sensitive sources and methods?

Interestingly, in the thing that the head of the National Intelligence put out, CIA and FBI are "highly confidential," and the NSA—now if there is real evidence—unless we have a source in the Kremlin, which

National Security Agency headquarters, Fort Meade, Maryland.

I really don't think we do—if there's real evidence, NSA would have it, right? They only have "moderate confidence...," So that's the technical side.

Ross: Let me just read a quote for our viewers. This is from the report that came out of the Office of the Director of National Intelligence on January 6. It said, "We also assessed Putin and the Russian government aspired to help President-elect Trump's election chances when possible by discrediting Secretary Clinton"—as though she didn't do that herself—"and publicly contrasting her unfavorably to him. All three agencies agree with this judgment. The CIA and FBI have high confidence in this judgment. The NSA [who might have any of the evidence] has moderate confidence."

McGovern: Let me just finish on the sources and methods because it's really interesting. I think I can contribute something from my own experience. In 1986, there was a discotheque in Berlin that U.S. GIs frequented. I think it was in April, it was blown up by a big bomb. Two GIs were killed, several were wounded. About 100 Germans were wounded and a lot of U.S. civilians as well. A big blast, OK? Who did it?

We knew who did it. I'm not revealing any secrets right now, but we had an intercepted, encrypted Libyan message showing that the Libyan intelligence service did that. They were congratulating each other. Mission accomplished. We told President Reagan. President Reagan didn't waste a day, flew some bombers out of England and blew the hell out of the palace in Tripoli, killed one of Qaddafi's young daughters and made a real mess of things—so much so that there was a lot of consternation in the world at large. What's this U.S. President doing? How does he know it was the—? My God, why would the Libyans blow up a disco in Berlin? Come on! It got pretty tense, it got pretty bad, and Reagan was getting a real black eye throughout the world.

So he comes to us and says, "Where's that message?" So we showed him the message. "We got to give this to the press." Oh no, no, you don't understand Mr.

President—"sources and methods." The Libyans don't know that we're intercepting their messages, and even if they suspect we are, they don't know we can decode them—this encrypted stuff. So if you go ahead and do that [release the intercept], we won't be able to see what they're doing from this source [in future]. Reagan looked and he said, "I thought I told you to release that." We said, "Oh yes sir" and we released it, immediately. The world got the real deal. Did we blow the source? Yeah, we blew the source, but there are some junctures at which the national interest is far better served by blowing a source—you're national interest is better served by coming out, showing where the beef is, where the evidence is and sacrificing other sources. That worked. It worked like clockwork. That's a good example of what is necessary now—assuming—now, this is a big assumption [that they have such sources]. I think I told you before, I'm 90 percent certain they don't have any sources, and if you read this drivel, God, it's embarrassing.

Let's say they did have an NSA source, one question is why are they only "moderate"? Let's say they have an NSA source, don't you think they should release that now? What makes them reluctant to do that? It's a canard. Particularly when the McCainiacs and others are saying this is an act of war. "Mr. Director, don't you think this is an act of war?" And the Director of National Intelligence starts to say, "Well, this is beyond my pay grade to tell you it's an act of war, but I think..." Anyhow, If it is an act of war, then we ought to really see what the evidence is.

Bill Binney and the rest of our group in Veteran Intelligence Professionals for Sanity, of which there are about fifty now—there isn't one who has said, "Hey, you know, maybe they do have something that they just can't possibly—maybe they have a guy sitting next to Putin, or maybe that beautiful woman is a 'hot off the press' spokesman. She does a great job for Lavrov, but maybe she's really working..." Come on!

So, the "sources and methods" is the only thing they have now, and it was interesting in today's *Washington Post* that David Ignatius, who is well plugged into all this says, "well obviously it is the sources and methods thing. It would be so great if they could reveal these things." In the Bronx where I come from, we call that a "crock."

The Corruption of U.S. Intelligence

Now the other thing of course is much more serious.

People don't realize that not only did Clapper lie to the Senate Intelligence Committee about NSA's coverage. You remember that wonderful picture where Wyden asks him, "Are you collecting information on millions or many millions of Americans?" And he's like he's looking for some hair, he says, "No. No sir." Then he thinks, "Oh my God." "Not advertently or inadvertently, or yeah, inadvertently we might—"

Ross: Not wittingly.

McGovern: You got it. Okay. "Not wittingly but inadvertently maybe we did." So then of course, that was March 12, 2013. So in June, Ed Snowden comes out and you could hear from the director of National Intelligence office all the way down to Virginia where I live, you know, he goes "Oops!" So, he writes a letter. It doesn't even go to the Senators. He writes a letter and he says "You know, what I said was clearly erroneous," that kind of thing.

Ross: I'd like to amend my testimony here.

McGovern: But what I wanted to tell you is that he's actually—all kidding aside—he's guilty of heinous malfeasance, not misfeasance, but malfeasance in office.

When Rumsfeld came in with George Bush and wanted to do a war in Iraq, he needed to gin up some evidence. It was easy to lean on George Tenet, the head of the CIA—he's a guy from Queens, I'm a guy from the Bronx. He got to play with the big boys, you know. If you get to play with the big boys, you got to know who the big boys are. So, Rumsfeld says, "Look, we're having a cabinet meeting. Show some pictures of some of those suspected chemical weapon facilities. So, Tenet says, "OK." The first cabinet meeting, Condoleezza Rice says, "George has some photos," and we know this because Paul O'Neill, Secretary of the Treasury at the time, was there. Okay? And he says, "I could hardly see anything at all, and I said what is this?" Tenet says those are suspected chemical weapon facilities. "Where?" So, Tenet pointed to a cloud or something. Tenet was easy.

Now how do you get the people who analyze satellite photography—now, realize, most people know this, but maybe not—when we put those satellites up for billions and billions of dollars, they take imagery. Not only photos, but infrared, radar, multispectral—this is fancy stuff. So they're going around here like this, and they're collecting all this stuff and of course they are fixated on Iraq because people say they have weapons of mass destruction.

Now Rumsfeld is a little bit worried about who he put in charge of imagery analysis, and so he picked a guy named James Clapper. The point of the background here is very sorrowful. Up until 1996, imagery analysis was done in a nonpartisan objective way, by folks whose expertise wouldn't quit. It was called the National Photographic Interpretation Center. It was the people who found the missiles in Cuba, it was the people that told not only Reagan but Nixon, "Look you conclude these arms control agreements, we can verify—you can trust." These are real professionals. Their average experience was about twenty-five years.

In 1996, the head of the CIA, John Deutch, who made it clear when he came to the CIA that this was just a stopping point, before he'd take the place of his old friend, Bill Perry, as Secretary of Defense. Right? All of a sudden, it was decided not to give this to Deutch; but before that was decided, Deutch said, "Well, how do I ingratiate myself with the Pentagon?" He had been Deputy there. So, he said, "I know what I'll do. I'll give our imagery analysis capability to the Pentagon. The Pentagon has a big role in collecting this stuff, they pretty much run the satellites, so why don't we give them the analysis function, as well?"

Now that's a no-no. That's for the CIA. That's for people who have no axes to grind. Those are people who can't be under a military regime. They have to act as civilians in the way that they did when they were verifying arms control agreements.

So that went, kit and caboodle; all 800 of these specialists in 1996 went to the Defense Department. There they are in something called the National Geospatial-Intelligence Agency (NGA). Now these are the people who might find the weapons of mass destruction in Iraq, or they might not find them—because they might not be there. So, Rumsfeld has this challenge. He says, "Jim" (James Clapper was an Air Force General), "look, you take charge of the NGA. You know the drill."

Put yourself in the position of somebody working for James Clapper. All through 2000, 2001, 2002, you have this steady stream of Iraqi émigrés—Ahmed Chalabi and his crew—and they're saying we know there's a chemical weapons facility at these coordinates right near Baghdad; or we know that there's a biological depot right here. So they give the coordinates to the NGA and the sergeant or the major who is looking at the

imagery says "that's a chicken coop" or that's a "gym for a high school." [laughter] Put yourself in the position of somebody who knows that James Clapper is going to get really, really mad if you pour cold water on these émigrés. If you say "Ahmed Chalabi doesn't know what the hell he's talking about or maybe he's fabricating; some of these Iraqis are really clever, they do fabricate stuff." Well, you wouldn't let any of that stuff through. *So the prime source for weapons of mass destruction was stifled,* by a guy named James Clapper.

Nobody knows that story, or maybe they do, but they just don't want to tell it. There he was! In the position of either verifying that there were weapons of mass destruction—the primary source—or saying no, there weren't any. And there weren't any—but nobody could say that.

So what happens? They find out there aren't any weapons of mass destruction. What does Jim Clapper say? "Oh! I think they moved them to Syria." [laughter] I mean, he had no evidence to support that, but that's what he said, "They moved them Syria"! So you see what I mean about not being the sharpest knife in the drawer? I mean, hallo-oo! And he got away with it, because the press—I haven't made this point yet, but I always try to make it: I've been in Washington for fifty-three years now; that's a long time. I've seen a lot of change, you see a lot of change in fifty-three years, but there's one change that dwarfs all the other changes. It's a sad change, and it's simply that we no longer have, in any real sense, a free media. That's big. The fourth estate is dead. I watched it die over Iraq. You could see it now, in this incredible drumbeat over Russians hacking, without any evidence, and so that's the bad news. Now, there is good news, and that is, that the young people I talk to, they don't buy that! [laughter] They don't even look at it on the Web! If they're smart enough, they can find what's going on, on what I call the fifth estate, which is on the Web.

So this past weekend, I had this terrible flashback, where I'm reading all this stuff, about the Russian hacking, the Russian hacking, the Russian hacking. On Saturday, the whole front page of the *New York Times* had a banner headline, like all eight columns, "Putin Behind Hacking of blah, blah, blah, Report Says." Now, my God! They're talking about this thing here.

You know, it's sad. Because I gave twenty-seven years to that. I used to chair National Intelligence Estimates, I used to brief Presidents with the President's Daily Brief. We took great pride in our work. It became corrupted under Bill Casey and Bobby Gates. When Ronald Reagan came in, Bill Casey was the director of the CIA under Reagan; and Bobby Gates—he's known as Robert Gates, Secretary of Defense, but he worked for me. [laughs] Interesting thought—he worked for me in the 1970s. I was chief of the Soviet foreign policy branch and I had him working on the Soviet policy in the Middle East. He was a bright guy, but he was so ambitious! He'd curry favor with my boss and his boss, and the first day he was there he asked how long it took my boss to get to where he is and all that stuff. So, he was a disruptive influence in the branch.

Ten years later Gates is in charge of *all* the analysis, under Bill Casey! Now, Bill Casey was the kind of guy, he was a really good spy guy for World War II, but he wasn't real sophisticated. He thought, for example, down in Nicaragua, that there was a Russian under every rock. You know, you turn over the rock, and this is a metaphor here, but Bobby Gates thought, you know, "Mr. Casey? You see that Russian? I see three Russians under this rock." That's an exaggeration, but just a little bit.

So Gates gets appointed by Casey to be the head of analysis. What happens? This is important, because only the people who would see two or three Russians under every rock, got a dance. And so who became head of the Soviet analysis part of the whole analysis? Somebody who didn't know anything about the Soviet Union but was a malleable manager. So, if Bobby Gates said, as he did, the Communist Party of the Soviet Union will never, ever give up power without a big struggle; and this Gorbachov fellow, he's just a Commie, man! He's just a Commie, he's just a more clever Commie, making all these noises. Don't trust them, they'll never give up power."

So we've got all these people coming in, and they're more interested in advancing their careers than they are in telling the truth, and they get advanced up. Now, what do we make out of all of this? Well, because it takes about a generation to corrupt an institution. So that was 1981, when Bobby Gates came in and Bill Casey.

Fast forward to 2002: Bush wants to make a war in Iraq. He's got a malleable manager in George Tenet who's the head of the CIA at the time, and Tenet knows that there aren't any weapons of mass destruction in Iraq, and so Tenet's solution for that, was to keep his head way down, and not let anybody write about weapons of mass destruction in Iraq. If you'd been through

that time, you realize what a big *cause célèbre* this was.

Anyhow, Bush and Cheney say, we're going to get the Congress to approve our going into Iraq. And so they do; they ask the Congress to move this legislation forward, and Bob Graham [D-FL] who was head of the Senate Intelligence Committee says, well, what about these, do we have a National Intelligence Estimate on weapons of mass destruction? And George Tenet says, no we don't. "Why not?"

"Well, we're really busy!" So, these guys don't have much spine: Graham was going to say, "Oh, you're too busy," but Dick Durbin [D-IL] was by his side, and he said, "Bob! They want us to vote on a war, and they're not going to do an estimate? Tell him he's got to do an estimate!" Graham called him back; he says, "Uh, George, if you don't do an estimate we're not going support this legislation." Hang up.

Now, I wasn't there, but I know how these things happen: Tenet says, "Oh, damn." Goes to the White House, says, "we've successfully escaped the need to write an estimate, but now the jig is up; they won't move the legislation unless we do an estimate." White House tells them, "No problem! Just two conditions: One is, the estimate has to come out exactly as Dick Cheney said the situation was on the 26th of August." That was just three weeks before, in the big speech he made at the Veterans of Foreign Wars, saying Saddam Hussein was about to get a nuclear weapon and all that kind of stuff. "And it's got to be done in 10 days, because they want to get it out and up before we force Congress to vote on whether I should be permitted to make war in Iraq."

Long story short: George Tenet goes back to the Director's conference room, where I spent many hours during my career, and he's got his top managers around the table, but they're not the same kind of managers that existed in my day—they're careerists. They're people that Bobby Gates has put in these positions because they will say there's a Russian under every rock. And Tenet says: "Well, we have to do a National Intelligence Estimate on weapons of mass destruction. And there are two conditions, one is that it has to be done in 10 days; and the other is, the conclusions have to be what Cheney said in Nashville on Aug. 26th."

Now, if that had happened in my day, we would have said "Ha-ha-ha! You want...! [laughs] George, you're kidding, right?" And if he said he wasn't kidding, we would be out of that door. There might be a sucker or so who'd stay around, but he'd know that he'd had an insurrection. We don't do that kind of stuff, right?

But now, this is a generation later, right? He's got all these malleable managers around, "Yessir, ten days? We can do that!"—and out of that came the worst, the very worst estimate on record from the CIA or any U.S. intelligence agency, saying there were all manner of weapons of mass destruction, chemical and biological, they're just about to get a nuclear... It was just really awful!

This Iraq estimate was dishonest, it was fraud. And you don't have to take my word for it. After a five-year investigation by the Senate Intelligence Committee, Jay Rockefeller presenting their final report, which was bipartisan, Chuck Hagel, Olympia Snowe; so, in introducing the report, Rockefeller said: The evidence or the intelligence that was concocted before the war in Iraq was fraudulent; that some of it was nonexistent. Now, I want to ask you: What does nonexistent intelligence look like? Well, it looks like forgeries and stuff like that.

So, that's a long story, but I'm afraid that these guys are not only dishonest, and that's the word I would use, I think Julian Assange is quite right in saying this is dishonest; but they're not even literate. I mean this stuff about hacking and stuff—as if this is evidence!

Reforms

Ross: Let me ask you this: What kind of reforms do you think are in order? How do we get the intelligence community, the intelligence agencies back in shape? What's required?

McGovern: Character matters. You need some characters with character: You need a director who realizes what the job is, and the job has evolved in a way that Truman, who created the CIA never intended... If you want to reform the intelligence community, you have to have somebody with integrity; you have to have somebody who will fulfill the function that Truman created the Agency for—namely, to have an analysis outfit that reports directly to the President! Now that was the legislation in 1947-48. The CIA was not going to be under the Pentagon; the Pentagon always made the Russians out to be ten feet tall. It wasn't going to be under the State Department, because they're always justifying their policy; it was going to be somebody reporting directly to the President, somebody, ideally that would have an In Box full of everything that he or she needed.

We need somebody in charge of the CIA who realizes what its main mission is, to give the President unvarnished truth about things. I don't think anybody's doing that now. Matter of fact, many of the analysts have become little more than targeters. What do they do? They collect stuff from cell phones in Afghanistan, from neighbors who want to get rid of the neighbor they don't like; put it together, and "OK, drone operators, these guys are suspected terrorists." And it was Brennan who was at Obama's side during all this, and would meet with him on Tuesday mornings and go through this list.

Here's the President, you know, and I could imagine him also having also a legal pad because he's a lawyer, and Brennan gives him this list, and he says, "Oh, which ones are we going whack this week?" "Well, there's three—now, John, didn't you tell me that this Ahmad, that he had three little kids and a wife?"

"Yes, Mr. President, but we saw him having lunch with the daughter-in-law of a suspected terrorist."

"Look, John, I don't feel good about Ahmad, so let's put #3 down, and #6 we'll talk about it next week, and we'll move the others up. So, we'll still get five, but let's not whack Ahmad. And excuse me, John, but now I have to go have lunch with Michelle."

Some of these people are American citizens! I mean, there is a Fifth Amendment: "No one shall be deprived of life, liberty or property without due process"! And here's our President saying, "well, let's ask the Attorney General about that." And so, Holder goes to a pretty reputable law school, Northwestern in Chicago, and he says, "well, I'm going to tell you why it is we're entitled to whack American citizens: You see the Fifth Amendment does say 'no one shall be deprived of life, liberty or property without due process,' but it doesn't say '*judicial* process.' It only says, 'due process,' and so, we 'do do doo-doo process,' right here in the White House, thank you, very much."

It's *always* meant judicial process! And the Germans do have in their Constitution, that it has to involve the courts, and the Germans are doing our bidding by letting us do that stuff from Ramstein [airbase].

So these are things that are a profound disappointment to me, and I just hope, against hope perhaps, that things will get better after the 20th of January.

Ross: Ray McGovern, thank you very much.
McGovern: You're most welcome, Jason.

II. A Dialogue of Cultures

MANHATTAN CONFERENCE

'Inspire Each Citizen To Act for the Future'

by Dennis Speed

Jan. 17—An unusual two-day "congress" took place in New York City over the Jan. 14-15 Martin Luther King Day weekend. The mission of the gatherings, and of the discussions and interventions made therein, was to up-shift a two-year process, termed in November 2014 by Lyndon LaRouche "the Manhattan Project." LaRouche, economist, statesman, and former candidate for the United States Presidency, had made clear from the inception of the Manhattan Project that he wished to intervene into the Presidential system process by reinstat-

ing the idea of the federal republic of the United States, as Alexander Hamilton had constituted that United States in his four famous reports on manufacturing, credit, and the national bank.

LaRouche composed Four Laws which both summarize and advance that Hamiltonian Presidential system to a new level, insisting that the General Welfare of a society can only be advanced by developing its human creativity, leading to an increase in the productive powers of labor. A new technology, even a

EIRNS/Robert Wesser

John Sigerson conducting the Schiller Institute Chorus Jan. 15, at St. Joseph's Co-Cathedral in Brooklyn, New York. The concert was part of the Jan. 14-15 Manhattan Conference held in New York City over the Martin Luther King Day weekend.

fundamentally new source of power that changes a society's productive basis, is not enough in itself to develop it. It is rather the individual minds of the population as a whole and their development, which are, properly speaking, the only real "natural resources" of a human economy, and the true source of the increase in a society's physical wealth. The universal cultural development of human creativity is the bedrock of all economic progress and wealth, not "natural resources."

Creating the New Paradigm for Mankind

In her keynote address to the Saturday Conference, "Inaugurating A New Paradigm: the Dialogue of Cultures," Schiller Institute founder and head Helga Zepp-LaRouche said:

Founder of the Schiller Institutes, Helga Zepp-LaRouche, addressing the Manhattan Conference Jan. 14.

Once every nation knows the best expressions of the other one, I'm absolutely certain that all conflicts will disappear, and we will have a rich, universal culture consisting of many national expressions and traditions—but still being united by universal principles of art and science.

Now, the other dimension which must come to this dialogue of cultures, or dialogue of civilizations, is a look into the future, not only back to the best traditions, but a look to where mankind should be in 100 years, in 1,000 years from now. There, it is very clear that the natural next phase of evolution is space: travel, research, cooperation, and colonization of space. If you think that in the long arc of evolution, life developed from the oceans with the help of photosynthesis, to land. You had higher forms of species developing with higher forms of energy-flux density in their metabolisms. Eventually, man arrived. Man started to move from the rivers and ocean coasts inland, with the help of infrastructure, and opened up the landlocked areas. Now, we are at that point where the New Silk Road, becoming the World Land-Bridge, is completely at that phase of evolution.

So, the natural next phase of human evolution is the development of nearby space in the first period, and then further space travel as we develop the technologies to do so, with the help of fusion energy and similar technologies. Man

will expand in space, and then we will no longer be just an Earth-bound species, but we will be a cosmo-political species, if you wish. That will then lead to a completely new knowledge about the identity of the human species.

We are in that period of a real epochal change, a New Paradigm, where I am absolutely certain mankind is about to become adult.

The Schiller Institute and Helga LaRouche in particular have insisted that a "new cultural platform must simultaneously come into existence with a new economic platform." This is an important conception to highlight. The "New Silk Road" is not only a system of railways and waterways, but involves the revolutionary idea of developing the interiors of continents through the creation of transcontinental "development corridors." On 50-100 km of either side of the "trunk lines," cities and factories are to be located, shifting population centers inland and away from exclusive concentration along coastlines of continents. This is a fundamental, decisive shift in human culture—the beginning of the end of the imperial model of society.

The populations of these development-corridor urban centers will be increasingly heterogeneous, as were the populations that traveled and lived along the ancient Silk Road, which stretched throughout Asia, Africa, and Europe. To prepare to cooperate with China, Russia, India, and other nations (for example Brazil and South Africa, the other two BRICS nations), a corresponding "new cultural platform" must also be erected. This is not mere "cultural exchange." It is a sense of a corresponding human identity, identical in all people, which is displayed in their greatest cultural achievements.

For example, consider Albert Einstein's passionate outlook on creativity, as exemplified by his personal devotion to the performance of Classical music on the violin. Einstein contended that he often did his most important thinking by playing his violin. It was the spiritual preparation made available though the internal daily dialogue with Mozart and Bach that allowed Einstein to compose his greatest achievements in science. And Einstein's participation in singer/scholar Paul Robeson's campaign against the lynching of African-Americans in the South in the 1940s and 1950s, including his famous 1946 address at Pennsylvania's Lincoln University, flowed from that same creative source.

Shifting the "popular," that is to say, totally wrong, view of the historical role of the Classical artist—meaning the poet, or composer, or creative scientist—is an essential task if the United States citizenry expects to "seize the moment" now offered by the Presidential transition process, and the possibility of renewed human relations with Russia and China in particular. The great ideas of Schiller, Shakespeare, Beethoven, and others, and the artist's personal role, must shift from that of being what Percy Shelley, in his "A Defense of Poetry," termed "the unacknowledged legislators of the world," to that exemplified by Alexander Hamilton's role: an acknowledged, self-conscious creator in the forefront of the invention, together with George Washington, of the American Presidency.

Speaking earlier in her Saturday keynote, Zepp-LaRouche had stated:

> Naturally, if the United States would cooperate with Russia, and have a decent relationship with China, then naturally the entire game plan to have this unipolar world—or call it globalization, which is just another word for Anglo-American financial empire—would go out of the window. So, that is why they are trying to undo this election of Donald Trump, and you

EIRNS/Jason Ross

Ben Wang, Senior Lecturer in Language & Humanities at China Institute, addressing the Manhattan Conference Jan. 14.

can see very clearly it is a direct intervention by the British.

> So, therefore, it's not a question of party against party, or it's not a question of nation against nation. It is the old dying paradigm of the British Empire—which is synonymous with globalization—clearly reacting to the emergence of the New Paradigm. Now that New Paradigm, however, is already very strong, and it is moving very rapidly.

Chinese Culture and the American Mind

A "culture shock" of the most friendly and salutary variety was delivered to the audience of 120 persons by Ben Wang, a pre-eminent lecturer on—and translator of—Chinese Classical poetry. An audience member offered this assessment of what transpired:

> Ben Wang's talent is that he can put you in stitches laughing with a few words, and keep your attention for hours as he leads even the most ignorant of audiences to understanding and appreciating the greatness of Chinese Classical literature. He gave a short but impactful lecture on Saturday, excerpting two heptasyllabic couplets from two poems by one of the most famous and revered poets in Chinese history, Li Ba (701-763), who earned the reverent sobriquet of "the Celestial of Poetry." The first couplet, from "Tune of Clarity and Serenity"

(761-763), praises the beauty of woman, in this case, one of the most famous in Chinese history, Yang Gui Fei (the favorite imperial consort of the most powerful Tang Dynasty emperor). As Ben said, Li Ba's poetic words are entirely metaphorical and filled with subtlety. He followed that with a second heptasyllabic couplet from "Passing Parrot Isle," an island on the south Yangtze River, which sank in the 14th Century. This couplet, about nature, again showed the musicality and beauty that lies in Chinese poetry. Last, Ben showed us a Literati Painting by one of the most famous Literati Painters, Shi Tao (1642-1701), whose took Li Ba's poetry and rendered it in painting. Ben showed us how in Literati paintings, poetry, calligraphy and painting came together into a blend that is uniquely Chinese.

The audience was so intellectually aroused with the intellectual life exhibited in the two presentations, that they were provoked to think, and think deeply. No one left at the official conclusion of the event. Many talked for nearly an hour afterwards, expressing their astonishment at having "never been exposed" to this depth of thinking before.

Presidents Lincoln, King, and LaRouche

The United States Presidential system, and the successful functioning of the Executive branch of government of our republic, demands a culturally literate citizenry capable of holding the Presidency accountable for the General Welfare. The recent actions of civil rights veteran and Congressman John Lewis, and others, miss the point entirely. An insistence that the Glass-Steagall reinstatement measure be passed by the Trump Administration as the first order of business, in the name of Martin Luther King Jr., and in the name of the actions that Lewis himself had taken in the cause of justice in the 1960s, would be the "Lincolnesque"—and Presidential—way to address the new Administration. That action can still be taken, and should be; the mistake can be rectified. The cultural flaw, and delusion, of "partisan politics" can and must be corrected.

The Rev. Dr. Martin Luther King, Jr., whom LaRouche has previously described as "the man who was most fit to be President" in the 1960s, demonstrated precisely this command of knowledge of the intent of the Constitution of the United States. King grasped Alexander Hamilton's idea of the Presidency and the General Welfare clause, as is best seen in his opposition to the war in Vietnam. His conscience demanded that he upgrade his earlier accomplishments in the field of "civil rights," to admonish the nation, including then-President Johnson, that the pursuit of the war violated the mission of the American Presidency, and he, King, was speaking out on behalf of that Presidency—not Johnson. On all important matters, King's theological and literary allusions were an essential part of his mode of thinking, his artist's view—that is, his higher mastery of the principles of the American Constitution.

What Lyndon LaRouche has termed "Politics As Art," is a conception and practice that is today foreign to most Americans. Yet, it was not always so. Abraham Lincoln's habit of reading and quoting from Shakespeare's tragedies during Cabinet meetings was an essential feature of his successful campaign to provide, from Shakespeare, those conceptions actually necessary to prosecute the war required to advance and perfect the United States republic, thus ending slavery. Therefore, because Lincoln was himself a poet, as can be seen from his Gettysburg Address and his Second Inaugural Address, he could recognize what the abolitionists could not: He recognized that by seeking to perfect the Union, one could end slavery, but by seeking to abolish slavery, one would not perfect the Union. Frederick Douglass agreed with Lincoln on this, which is why Douglass not only rejected John Brown, but successfully collaborated with Lincoln in enlisting 200,000 African-American males into military service in 1863, providing the decisive military component that in fact ended the war, and slavery.

The Martin Luther King Jr. Weekend allowed the Schiller Institute, which has held conferences or commemorations of King's birthday each year for thirty-one years, to also point out that King, like Lincoln, is an international, not merely American, figure. King's visit to Berlin on Sept. 13, 1964,—where he addressed more than 20,000 people and said, "Where people break down the dividing wall of hostility which separates them from their brothers, Christ achieves his ministry of reconciliation,"—may be unknown to Americans, but will never be forgotten by the Germans (and the Americans) who were there.

As with Lincoln and King, but in an even more extreme way, Lyndon LaRouche's launching of the set of ideas which gave birth to what is today called the "World Land-Bridge" or "New Silk Road," first at the Kempinski Hotel in Oct. 12, 1988, and again on Nov. 10, Schiller's Birthday, in 1989, is, together with the complete coverup of LaRouche's role in the 1983 Strategic Defense Initiative, the most suppressed fact of the last fifty-three years of American history, post-Kennedy assassination (and the derivative assassinations of Malcolm X, King, and Robert Kennedy). This topic was discussed by Helga Zepp-LaRouche in the answer to a question posed by John Sigerson, music director of the Schiller Institute. [See accompanying article.]

It is not necessary for an American to actually be elected to the Presidency to affect, in a fundamental way, the Presidential system. Hamilton was never President, nor was Martin Luther King Jr., nor was Lyndon LaRouche. As with Joan of Arc, however, the power of that office can also speak through the voice of the una nointed citizen inspired to fulfill that Presidential mission. That is what makes the practice of American citizenship the most powerful position in the world, when people have the eyes of a Schiller, King, Lincoln, or LaRouche to see themselves thus.

Sending the Best Message from America To China and Russia

Jan. 17—*The following exchange between John Sigerson and Helga Zepp-LaRouche took place at the Jan. 14 Manhattan Conference.*

John Sigerson: Hi. For those people who don't know me, I'm John Sigerson, music director of Schiller Institute.

The hysteria around the Russian hacking strongly reminds me of the situation in 1986, when two LaRouche activists won the Democratic primaries for Lieutenant Governor and Secretary of State in the state of Illinois. That unleashed a furor where every single media outlet picked up the lie, that it was

Lyndon LaRouche and his associates who were responsible for the recent assassination of the Swedish Prime Minister Olof Palme. And it was truly incredible, the Big Lie that happened then. I just wanted to point that out.

But to get to my main question, I was recently in Washington meeting with congressional staffers, and in the process of that, I think I figured out what the big roadblock in Congress is. [laughter] In the remaining banter in the process of these meetings, I pointed out that I would be very interested in,— I was pointing out that it would be very nice to found some kind of a chorus amongst the congressional staffers and maybe the congressmen and the senators themselves; because they really don't have anything like that. And in every single case, the staffer whom I was talking with said, "Well, that sounds like a wonderful idea, but I can't sing"!

So I think that in the process of learning to sing, we might be able to make some real progress.

But coming back to these meetings more seriously, what I was doing was briefing the staffers on the two events that we had here in Manhattan and in New Jersey, commemorating and giving condolence to the Russian people for the deaths of ninety-two people, including the large majority of the Alexandrov Ensemble, who were on their way in a jet plane to Syria.

For those people who don't know, that jet went down on our Christmas Day. A number of days afterward, the Schiller Institute participated in a wreath-laying ceremony at the Russian consulate here in Manhattan, and we sang, in Russian, the Russian National Anthem. And this video went completely viral on Russian Internet media, resulting in nearly 500,000 views and a flood, an outpouring of comments from Russians, thanking us for showing that there are Americans who really don't believe in this crazy hysteria that's going on.

And then later, on Jan. 7, which happens to be the Russian Orthodox Christmas, we held a wreath-laying ceremony at the famous Tear Drop Monument [in Bayonne, New Jersey], in collaboration with many organizations, including most prominently the New York City Police Department. This monument had been contributed by the Russians to commemorate 9/11.

I pointed out to the congressmen and their staffers that what is really required, in all of the things that we do right now, including the adoption of Glass-Steagall and other things, is that it's not so much a question of what we do, specifically—the legislation that we pass—but rather the intention behind what we do, and that the kind of messages that, say, Valery Gergiev gave when he went to Palmyra, to perform in a city in Syria which had just been recently liberated from the ISIS terrorists, and these kinds of gestures, are absolutely necessary in order to send a message to the Russians and to the Chinese, that indeed there is an intention in the United States to collaborate, and that that is actually what China and Russia are waiting for.

And I would like you to comment on that, and on giving any idea of other kinds of messages that the American population and the American Congress can send to China and Russia, to give this sense that there's really going to be a change and that we can really do this. Thank you.

Helga Zepp-LaRouche: Well, there are obviously many things one can think of. But since you mentioned the 1986 parallel, which is really absolutely to the point, I would like to answer the question in the following way:

What Trump is now experiencing is really what I would call "the LaRouche treatment." Because, my husband, who is very well known to many of you—he was a Presidential candidate several times—and the way he was treated by the United States, including his illegal and criminal incarceration by the Bush family,—I still think that because of this criminal campaign against him, the American people have been deprived of the most beautiful and most important ideas expressed by any living American in our time. The fact that the United States is today in such terrible condition, with a shrinking life-expectancy, with an increased suicide rate, alcoholism, drug epidemics,—all of this is the result of the fact that because of this campaign committed by the Bush apparatus, the American people could not clearly look at these ideas and adopt them. And the United States would be quite a different place today, if this had not happened.

Now, the difference is, in the case of LaRouche, the British Empire and their British puppets in the United States were able to carry this out clandestinely, in the way that spooks operate, with fake news. What you

EIRNS/Jason Ross

John Sigerson, Schiller Institute Music Director, at the Manhattan Conference on Jan. 14.

mentioned about the so-called Palme assassination was a classical case of fake news, but there were many, many other fake news stories around LaRouche as well. And I think the best message to be sent—because there is a different America—would be that if this attack on Trump which is now occurring, not clandestinely, but it is all out in the open!... The British Empire is personally showing its hand. Christopher Steele, MI6, former British ambassadors, are all openly speaking.

So it is really the time to straighten out history: You know, America was made against that British Empire. The American Revolution was a revolution against that British Empire which has subverted the American establishment and convinced the elites to rule the world as an empire based on the Anglo-American "special relationship."

Now the only way people in the rest of the world will have confidence that the United States is again becoming a republic, is if this goes together with the rehabilitation of Lyndon LaRouche. Because I do not think this injustice which was done—and you'll permit me to say it, because I'm saying it because I'm his wife, but I'm also saying it in the full estimate of his personality—if the rightful place of Lyndon LaRouche were acknowledged by forces inside the United States, it would be the best message for China and for Russia, because it would prove that people are becoming serious.

Confucius Comes to Washington

by William Jones

Jan. 16—The China National Opera and Dance Drama Theater brought its dance drama about the life of the great Chinese philosopher Confucius to the nation's capital at the Kennedy Center Opera House on Jan. 13. Without a doubt, it is an appropriate time to perform the ballet here in Washington, since we are on the verge of a new Administration.

The main topic of the life and work of Confucius was the issue of governance, not in the rather trivial sense the term is bandied about in political jargon these days, but rather in governance in the more profound sense of preserving the fabric of society in which, as Cicero wrote, the good of the people is the supreme law of the land.

Confucius (551-479 BC) lived during what is known as the Warring States Period, before China was unified (221 BC). This was a period in which China was divided into numerous states, which often conducted wars against each other, whether seeking more territory, more wealth, or simply retribution for previous alleged grievances.

Confucius traveled the length and breadth of most of what is today's China, seeking a ruler who would adhere to his notions of proper governance and benevolence. Except for some limited and transitory successes, he never really found a government willing to make his principles the basis of governing. At the end of his life, he returned to his home in the state of Lu, where he continued to teach his disciples, and wrote his books describing the lessons that he had tried to teach to the leaders of the various states.

When he died, he may have felt that his work had been a failure, but in fact the lessons he taught and the

Statue of Confucius at Confucian Temple in Shanghai, China.

writings he left behind became the basis of Chinese thinking for well over two millennia, and make themselves felt in Chinese policy and practice to this day.

The ballet drama was sparse with words. In fact no words were spoken until the final act. The drama depicted the life of Confucius. While there were larger groups of dancers performing in the various scenes, as soldiers, attendants, or ladies-in-waiting, there were four main characters:

- Confucius, played by Hu Yang,
- the Duke, played by Zhu Yin,
- the Concubine, played by Tang Shiyi, and
- the Duke's Minister, played by Guo Haifeng.

The drama begins with a prelude in which a group of dancers perform an exquisite plume dance to recall their deceased teacher and philosopher. The figure of Confucius stands with his back to us in the shadows, until he is called forth to begin his mission, beginning in Act 1, labeled "The Chaotic Time." Confucius approaches the Duke with a scroll on which he has written his tenets of governance, but the Duke, more taken with the beauty of the Concubine than with matters of state, refuses to meet with the philosopher or even read his scroll. The Duke's Minister treats Confucius roughly, and angrily throws the scroll down.

Finally, Confucius approaches the Concubine with his scroll. She is moved by what Confucius has written, and tries to persuade the Duke to accept the doctrine of Benevolence that is being propounded by Confucius. The Duke's Minister, however, sensing the danger to him of this alliance of his Duke with the doctrines of Confucius, plots to carry out a coup

The dance drama Confucius

against the Duke, in which he succeeds.

The next scene, titled "Out of Food," shows the starving people in a land now devastated by war and famine. The Minister, now in charge, comes to distribute food in a haughty manner aimed at winning the obedience of the masses. Confucius responds angrily, and refuses to accept food handed out with contempt. During a blizzard, Confucius continues to play his zither and to sing, full of optimism. He continues to lecture his disciples and teach his doctrines. The beautiful melodies tend to transport him into a beautiful dreamland.

In this state, Confucius, in Act III entitled "Great Harmony," compares a gentlemen of virtue to a piece of jade, cordial and gentle. Large jade figures are brought on the stage, around which the groups of dancers swirl. Confucius even dreams that the Duke has awarded him a sword as a symbol of respect and honor, and performs a beautiful sword dance in joy at his success.

But then reality intervenes. In Act IV, "Mourning for Benevolence," people have been plunged into an abyss of misery, and death is everywhere. Confucius wanders alone, lost and helpless. Then he imagines his mother bringing him a lighted candle to warm his path of spiritual exploration. Cherry blossoms descend slowly, depicting his beautiful homeland. Melody fills the air while an orchid blossom appears, a flower which flourishes even in inclement weather. Confucius hopes that, once noticed by the rulers, it might diffuse its fragrance to the world.

In the last scene, "Epilogue: Happiness," Confucius is back in his hometown, devoting his life to educating his disciples and compiling the Six Classics: the *Classic of Poetry*, the *Book of Documents*, the *Book of Rites*, the *Classic of Music*, the *I Ching*, and the *Spring and Autumn Annals*, books that would form the basis of Chinese culture for over two millennia.

In the final scene, the dancers are gathered on stage reciting sayings of Confucius in unison, which are translated on a monitor for English-speakers:

• "When one sees a virtuous man, one should think of exerting oneself to be like him";

• "When one sees someone who is not virtuous, one should examine oneself";

• "People know it better who work on it, but not as well as those who love it";

• "He who does not think of the future is certain to have immediate worries";

• "In the face of benevolence, do not give precedence even to your teacher"; and

• "If I learned the Way in the morning, I can die content in the evening."

EIRNS/William Jones
Hu Yang, as Confucius

EIRNS/William Jones
Tang Shiyi, as the Concubine

EIRNS/William Jones
Guo Haifeng, as the Minister

While encompassing the life and works of a great philosopher in dance and music only, without words, may seem a daunting task, the China National Opera and Dance Drama Theater succeeded masterfully in accomplishing it.

The dancing and the music were exquisite. In particular, Tang Shiyi, who played the Concubine, was almost acrobatic in her agility, combining it with grace and beauty to such an extent that it seemed almost effortless. In addition, the noble elegance in the dance movements of Hu Yang as Confucius, reflected well the grandeur of character of the great philosopher.

EIRNS/William Jones
Kong Dexin, choreographer of Confucius

One of the surprising aspects of the dance drama was that it was choreographed by a young lady, Kong Dexin, a 77th-generation direct descendant of Confucius (Kong Qiu, in Chinese). She is very proud of her family history, and first presented *Confucius* in 2013 in Beijing. "Each person has to go through hardships to reach the prime moment of his or her life," Kong Dexin told *China Daily* after the performance of *Confucius* in New York on Jan. 9. "So did Confucius. I think my drama, to some extent, brings him from the altar of worship, to the world in which ordinary people are living. I want to show spectators the uneasy part of his life," she said.

She explains how the drama's theme song, "Virtues of the Silent Orchid," was inspired by a poem written by Confucius. "When Confucius was traveling across various kingdoms, he saw orchids blossoming silently amidst the grass by the roads. He thought about himself, and he wished he could grow like those orchids. Many of our spectators cried when they listened to the theme song," she said.

An interesting personal touch to the performance was that the performers and the choreographer came out directly from the performance to the lobby of the Kennedy Center to sign the programs of the enthusiastic audience.

The fact that these concepts were brought to a large Washington audience at this moment of transition, may help serve as a sign that "business as usual" is no longer an option, since such a policy will only lead to tragedy. The alternative is the concept of "win-win" cooperation, which has been continually reiterated by Chinese President Xi Jinping. This approach provides the only way of conducting policy that reflects a sense of benevolence toward the people.

The visit of *Confucius* may have some effect on the governance of our nation, if only by creating greater interest among those who were touched by the three performances here in Washington and at Lincoln Center in New York, and by getting observers to take a closer look at the works of Confucius, as part of an attempt to gain a greater understanding of the rich culture out of which the Chinese nation emerged. Let us take the valuable lessons Confucius gave to the world, and use them to transform the destiny of mankind toward a condition in which Benevolence becomes the norm.

III. From Earlier Breakthroughs of Lyndon LaRouche

EIR will be reprinting earlier papers of Lyndon H. LaRouche, Jr., to familiarize readers with his discoveries.

TODAY'S NUCLEAR BALANCE OF POWER

The Wells of Doom

by Lyndon H. LaRouche, Jr.

This EIR *Strategic Studies analysis, written Dec. 10, 1997, was published in* EIR *Volume 24, Number 51, on Dec. 19, 1997.*

Dec. 10, 1997—Of "information society," let it be said: Once more, this recent October, an "unsinkable Titanic" was fatally holed by its col-liaison with the waiting, relevant species of iceberg. The impregnable post-1989, globalized financial system, is now settling into the watery abyss. Unfortunately, sanity being what it is, or is not, these days, even after the global events of October and November, most of the passengers, including former Citibank chief Walter Wriston, are still clinging to the sinking ship, clinging to a delusory faith in an "unsinkable utopia," in an "eternal, neo-Malthusian, information society's" economy.[1]

"Yes, there seem to be some ups and downs on the markets," is the gist of most U.S. adults' reluctant acknowledgment of the recent several weeks of global financial storms; "but," they add, "the economy is still basically sound. They would never let it happen here. Until I see it announced on television, I am not going to let myself believe, that that sort of crisis will ever come here." Although the modern Manichean, that citizen, leaves unclear, who, or what these mysterious potencies, "they," might be, the impression is, that they are awesomely Olympian.

Such popular superstition put to one side, given the catastrophes to the global financial system since late October through early December, no economist or political figure anywhere on this planet, could still be excused for believing a U.S. daily news media which promises that the current Asia crisis will never spread into the U.S. economy. After such events, no professional could still honestly deny the exceptional accuracy of my published, February 1997 forecast: an outbreak of a global, systemic financial crisis, beginning no later than October 1997.[2] The recent seismic shocks to the world's financial system, have assumed the form of an eerie drum-beat; from Asia, through Europe, and into the Americas, the situation has become constantly worse. Until certain key governments end the presently ongoing attempts, to "bail out" a sinking financial Ti-

---

1. Walter Wriston, address to the Cato Institute, as broadcast on C-Span 2 on Dec. 3, 1997. (See *Documentation,* in this issue.)

2. During February 1997, the present writer disseminated a series of warnings, in various published interviews, and otherwise, warning that 1997 would be a year of a grave international financial crisis. He indicated the 4th Quarter of 1997 as the outer limit for eruption of such a crisis, warning people to shift from speculative financial investments, such as futures and mutual funds, into long-term U.S. Treasuries, and actual ownership of gold, even if nominal losses had to be expected in the short- to medium-term on such changes in investment holdings. (For example, in a radio interview with "**EIR** Talks," Feb. 5: "Sure, Treasuries don't yield as much, but you've got one advantage with Treasuries: the government has agreed to back them up, and you've got something. Whereas, on these indexes, these futures, these options, when that market goes, you've got less than nothing.") During the Spring months, he updated that February warning, warning that a mild or severe shock could be expected by August, but that a heavy shock was virtually certain for October. (For example, to "**EIR** Talks," June 17: "The talk is, the recognition now, is that this past crisis, the March-April and the upcoming one which will land here, expectedly, from Mars or something, between June, late June, and Oct. 31, the end of the third quarter kind of thing, that that will be a lollapalooza. Not necessarily the big one, but it forces us to look at the fact that the big one is coming."

H.G. Wells was the first publicist of the argument of a "nuclear balance of power," and also a key figure in shaping what would become the rock-drug-sex counterculture. "Wells," writes LaRouche, "like the Dick Morris who did so much to sink the U.S. DemocraticParty's 1996 campaign for the U.S. House of Representatives, typifies the use of the pimp as a publicist."

tanic, whose bottom has already been ripped out irreparably, the crisis will become worse, world-wide, that at an accelerating rate.

Meanwhile, as if to show us that matters were not already as bad as they might become, the policies demanded by both thuggish U.S. Federal Reserve Chairman Alan Greenspan and IMF Managing Director Michel Camdessus, for example, have already begun what threatens to become, very quickly, a hyperinflationary spiral, like that which struck Weimar Germany during 1922-1923 [**Figures 1** and **2**]. The difference is, that, if this Weimar-1923-style policy of Greenspan and Camdessus were continued throughout Asia, and into the oncoming explosions in Russia, and South America, the result must be a Weimar-style hyperinflation, which might reach total breakdown, world-wide, not over months, as in 1922-1923, but, because of the added impact of a global, $100 trillions-equivalent "derivatives" bubble, compressed into a period as short as weeks.

In such economics matters, mere statistical studies may inform us of such relevant considerations, such as the fact that the patient is dead, but they provide little help in defining the cures which might have saved the economy, if not its financial system. If we wish to cure the disease, we must go behind the mere symptoms, to identify the agency which those symptoms express. To discover the cure, we must discover the source of the sickness. To find the continuing source of this global civilization's sickness, the presently onrushing, systemic, global financial crisis, we must focus upon the pattern of decisions which continue, even today, to shape economic practice: not the mere statistical effects of that practice. It is the substance of Genghis Khan, not his statistical shadow, which constitutes the mortal threat to our civilization. In short, to overcome the danger, the U.S. government must reverse the policy-trend of the recent thirty-odd years.

What must be introduced, would be considered by today's commonplace, elected illiterates in the subject

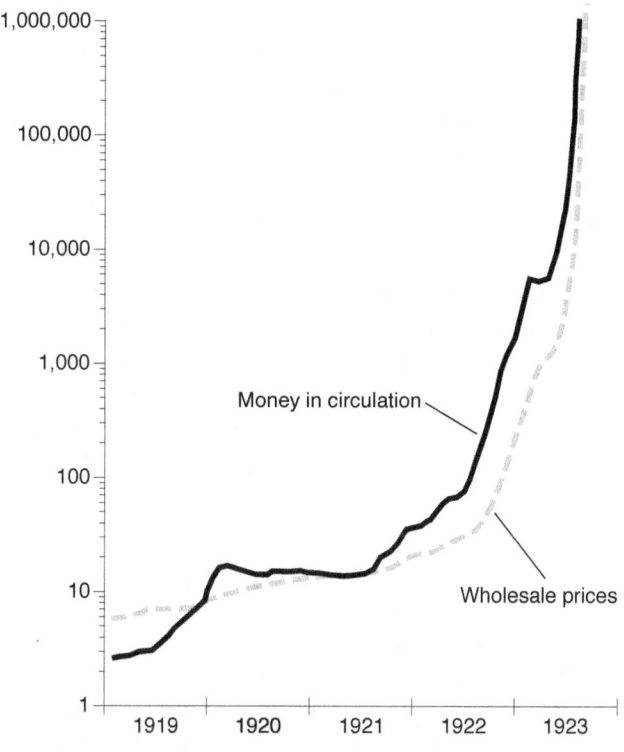

FIGURE 1

Germany and hyperinflation, 1921-23

(index 1913 = 1)

Money in circulation

Wholesale prices

Source: Knut Borchardt, "Wachstum und Wechsellagen 1914-1970," in Hermann Aubin and Wolfgang Zorn (eds.), *Handbuch der deutschen Wirtschafts- und Sozialgeschichte,* Stuttgart: Klett, 1976, vol. 2, p. 699.

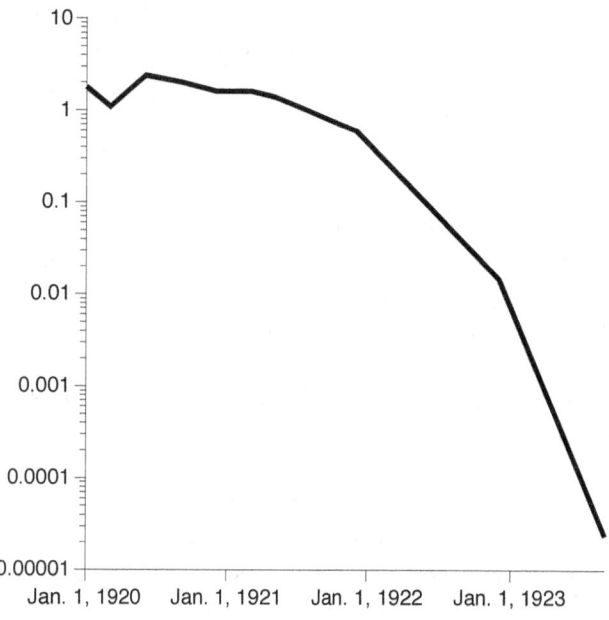

FIGURE 2

Hyperinflation, Germany, 1921-23

(value of German mark in U.S. cents)

Source: Stephen V.O. Clarke, *Central Bank Cooperation, 1921-31* (Federal Reserve Bank of New York, 1967).

Once the printing presses in Weimar Germany were turned on full throttle, the mark went into a free fall relative to the U.S. dollar. At the end of 1919, the mark was worth 1.8¢. It remained in that trading range through the second quarter of 1921, when it exchanged for 1.4¢. Then, the hyperinflationary process began. By November 1921, the mark had tumbled to 0.6¢, a fall of 57% from its second-quarter level. By November 1922, its worth was 147 ten-thousands of 1¢. By the end of the third quarter of 1923, it had depreciated to 238 ten-millionths of 1¢. Since mid-1921, about 99.99% of the value of the mark, relative to the dollar, had vanished.

of economics history, such as Speaker Newt Gingrich, as very radical changes in policies. If precisely those policies are not soon introduced, to deal with an already hopelessly bankrupt set of international financial and monetary institutions, this is a bottomless crisis. In the case those policies are not introduced very soon, this planetary civilization would be doomed, doomed by a lack of moral fitness to survive, doomed to plunge into the post-modernist barbarism of a prolonged "new dark age," even before the 2000 U.S. election-campaigns begin. Unless, we can detect and eradicate those policies and supranational institutions, which have caused the past thirty-odd years' decline in world economy, our culture is a dying culture, our nations, their populations, the casualties of a dying, global civilization.

Thus, modern European civilization, now somewhat more than six hundred years old, is, presently, dying. Nothing could save the present financial and monetary system itself. By the end of this century, perhaps sooner, it, in its present form, will be gone, either

by responsible actions of key governments, or, lacking that remedy, by way of either hyperinflationary, or hyperdeflationary collapse, forever. As my own and other features in ***EIR*** have repeatedly warned, this financial-monetary system is like a doomed, sinking ship; the passengers, the nations, the peoples, and the physical economy living within this civilization, could be saved, but only if they are willing to abandon that doomed ship itself. They could survive, but only if they give up, suddenly, those post-1964, radical changes in culture, which have doomed the present world economic order.[3]

---

3. The repeated comparison of the present crisis to the sinking of the *Titanic* is no less irony than a true *metaphor.* It was not the design of Britain's Titanic which was at fault; the ship was, in fact, better than most among those transatlantic passenger craft which were *not* sunk by icebergs that season. If the fault lay not in the design of the physical

Unfortunately, the prevailing evidence warns us, that no more than a small minority of the populations and their doomed governments are yet willing, to support the policies needed to allow our nations to survive that global systemic financial crisis which has recently entered its terminal phase. For the moment, the boob-tubed majority of the pleasure-seeking populations of Europe and North America—most notably—seem to have lost the will to grasp for anything but the next fleeting instant of momentary—or, should we better say, monetary—pleasure.

We must view the majority of the people of most nations today, as like the pompous, doomed Akkadians of Biblical Belshazzar's Babylonian empire; most of the leading institutions of this planet appear to have lost that essential quality, moral fitness to survive. So, as the artist portrayed a similar circumstance, Belshazzar's Feast:[4] once again, the moving finger writes; the new message is now nearly completed.

How did our world get into such a mess? When and how did we start down the road to this catastrophe? What habits must we rip out of our institutions, and ourselves, if we, and our republic are to survive the ongoing, terminal disintegration of the entire world's present financial and monetary systems?[5]

---

object, that ship, where, then, did the fault lie? Similarly, the present ruin of the world's economy was not the result of any flaw inhering in the pre-1964 model of the U.S. physical economy. Thus, the relevant metaphor of 1997's *Titanic* disaster is posed. Had not the owners, the captain, and induced British pride in the matter, insisted upon the false assumption that the doomed ship was the fastest, most unsinkable extant, neither the Company nor the captain would have committed the fatal errors of policy and command which sent the ship at its relatively highest cruising speed into a fully expectable iceberg. The cause of the ship's sinking was, thus, nothing other than the owner's, the captain's, and the British public's hysterical obsession with a set of purely ideological ruling assumptions. It was those perverse assumptions, the relevant mindset shaping the decisions, which, decision by decision, defined the tragic sequence of decisions leading toward doom, in both cases. The root of tragedy, in these cases, as on the stage of Aeschylus, Shakespeare, and Schiller, is a debate over decisions as such, which refuses to take into account the underlying, axiomatic assumptions, which are the actual mother of the decision leading to doom.

4. Rembrandt van Rijn, *Belshazzar Sees the Handwriting on the Wall* (c. 1636). *Belshazzar: Bel-shar-usse,* co-king of the doomed dynasty of Babylon, circa 538 B.C.
5. In other words, what was the "cultural paradigm-shift" involved? What was the change in underlying axiomatic principles of decision-making, which caused a previously upward-moving, increasingly collaborative international industrial society of the late Nineteenth Century, to change the effective direction of its decision, into becoming a Hobbesian collection of heteronomic gladiator-nations, plunged into two Great Wars, the age of nuclear balance of terror, and the suicidal insanity of the takeover of world decision-making by the sheer irratio-

To understand how all this occurred, how the most powerful civilization ever crafted, brought itself, like the fabled *Ozymandias,* to this present point of degradation and self-destruction, listen to a true story which begins with the Sept. 6, 1901 assassination of patriotic U.S. President William McKinley, by an imported terrorist protégé of New York's Emma Goldman's Henry Street Settlement House, Leon Czolgosz. The mortal wounding effected by this assassin's attack, an attack steered by self-anointed "tyrannicide" Goldman herself, brought a nasty spawn of the Confederacy, Theodore Roosevelt, into the U.S. Presidency, on Sept. 14, eight days later. About the same time, in England, a pathetic, perverse, but, subsequently, very influential British publicist, Herbert George Wells (1868-1946), escaped from what had been well-deserved obscurity. This Wells would later describe his personal acquaintance and ideological ally, Theodore Roosevelt, aptly, as "The Big Noise of America."[6]

That intersection of these two personalities, Wells and Theodore Roosevelt, with the accession of Prince Edward Albert as Britain's King Edward VII, typify a century gone wrong from the start, the century of 1) two World Wars, 2) a terrifying nuclear balance of power, which Wells was the first to propose publicly and widely, beginning 1914, and, 3) the recent thirty-odd years of worldwide reign of a global, neo-Malthusian nightmare, the latter another Wells dogma. These three factors, including the two dogmas, the one proposed, the other adopted by Wells, became, significantly through his contributing influence, the principal proximate cause of the presently ongoing worldwide economic-breakdown crisis.

Wells' Nuclear Balance of Power

In these and other ways, among literate historians and other relevant authorities on the matter, H.G. Wells has notable importance for our understanding the strategic, political, economic, and moral crisis now enveloping this planet. An unlikely candidate for fame and influence? He was, admittedly, like fellow Fabian tribesman George Bernard Shaw, essentially a shallow *poseur,* in the literal sense of the Latin derivation of "vanity": a miserable, invidious, misanthropic wretch, a picaresque eternal lout of immense vanity, of a personal character to be compared, and that not too favor-

---

nalism of a neo-Malthusian, "post-industrial" utopianism?
6. H.G. Wells, *An Experiment in Autobiography* (New York: MacMillan & Company, 1934), p. 646.

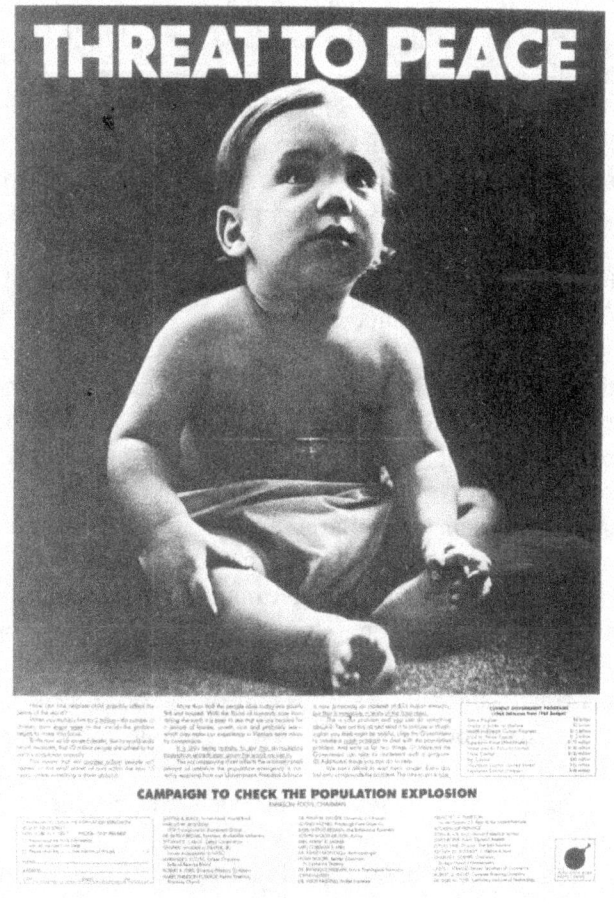

Neo-Malthusian propaganda in the 1960s (left) and the 1990s (right). H.G. Wells laid the foundations for this anti-human doctrine: "In a world where pressure on the means of subsistence was a normal condition of life, it was necessary to compensate for the removal of traditional sexual restraints, and so my advocacy of simple and easy love-making had to be supplemented by an adhesion to the propaganda of the Neo-Malthusians."

ably, with the popular image of a "mafia boss." He was, in short, exactly the sort of lackey the British oligarchy would employ and cultivate to do a particularly nasty bit of thuggery.

From the time of this English *Sparafucile*'s rocketing out of obscurity, at the beginning of this century, he is to be compared with the notorious textbook case of Typhoid Mary; like her, incontestably a figure who has, in his time, radiated a certain unpleasant influence. To appreciate Wells' high-ranking, and generally rising importance in relevant world events, during the interval 1901-1939, think of him as, like Adolf Hitler, or his fellow-criminal Bertrand Russell, a carrier of what has proven to be an extremely virulent strain of cultural syphilis.[7] Wells did not destroy our civilization by him-

self; but, he played a key, and exemplary part, as a tissue in which the relevant killer-strain of infection was cultured and disseminated.

Both Wells' depraved admirers and the populist's typically associative, Hobbesian view of a "world government conspiracy," treat Wells, and other lackeys of his type, as either admirable, or despicable geniuses. Wells was no genius; his talent was, as he implicitly describes himself, a man with a pimp's insight into the susceptibility of a depraved clientele's not-so-hidden private sexual fantasies.[8] In each case an influential idea is attributed to Wells, whether by devotees or de-

_____

7. Wells would acknowledge our choice of venereal disease, as an allusion to those utopian sexual fantasies, akin to those of degraded crea-

tures such as Carl Jung, Wilhelm Reich, and former President George Bush's employer, the Moon cult, which, according to Wells' plausible, autobiographical statement of the case, shaped his thinking about all the subjects of his work which we address here. See Wells, op. cit., pp. 392-409.

8. Wells, op. cit., pp. 392-409.

tractors, we discover that no such originality ever existed. His role was never that of a discoverer of principles; indeed, there is nothing of principle in Wells' vocabulary. Wells was not an inventor, but, rather, a publicist, a man like Dick Morris, the recently notorious cousin of the late Roy M. Cohn, a pathetic creature who turned his pimp's instinct for the sexual perversities of a general public, into a public-relations career.

This is a crucial point, so we should add a few more relevant observations on the distinction we have just made.

For example, Wells writes:

The *New Machiavelli*[9] is all the world away from overt eroticism. The theme . . . stressed the harsh incompatibility of wide public interests with the high, swift rush of imaginative passion—with considerable sympathy for the passion. . . . I was not indulging myself and the world in artistic pornography or making an attack upon anything I considered moral. . . . I was releasing, in these books, a long accumulation of suppression. I was working out the collateral problems with an ingenuous completeness. . . . In a world where pressure on the means of subsistence was a normal condition of life, it was necessary to compensate for the removal of traditional sexual restraints, and so my advocacy of simple and easy love-making had to be supplemented by an adhesion to the propaganda of the Neo-Malthusians. This I made in my *Anticipations* (1900)[10] and continued to write plainly on that subject in a period when Neo-Malthusianism was by no means the respectable movement it has become.[11]

The political function for which a publicist such as Wells, is subjected to a competitive process of selection, is to transform the ideas which the prospective employers intend to promote, into the easy form in which the mere name of such ideas can acquire pleasurable associations within a large ration, if not yet the majority, of a targetted population and the institutions which that population regards as expressing its self-interest.

_____

9. 1911.
10. *Anticipations of the Reaction of Mechanical and Scientific Progress upon Human Life and Thought* (London: Chapman and Hall, 1901).
11. *An Experiment in Autobiography,* pp. 398-399.

That is not the manner in which ideas *should* be given wider currency; the cognitive methods of Classical humanistic education, are the proper approach to all forms of education of a population, especially the population of a nation which wishes to escape the fall from republic to tyranny. Wells, like the Mephistopheles of Goethe's *Faust*, is a British empiricist, who avoids cognition; he targets the population's irrational susceptibilities, the target's non-cognitive, associative modes of fantasy-life: erotic imagery.

Wells, like the Dick Morris who did so much to sink the U.S. Democratic Party's 1996 campaign for the U.S. House of Representatives, typifies the use of the pimp as a publicist. "Run it up the flagpole, and see who salutes it!" "Throw it against the wall, and see if it sticks!" "Read the polls, and discover which of last night's political entertainments found their way into the polluted imageries of a relative majority of the targetted strata of the population." Hence, the use of Wells' policy of sexually-oriented utopian propaganda, in the case of the financially successful basing of the origins of the Promise Keepers' cult on the use of Jungian homoerotic imageries.[12]

That sort of pimp, like the mass-media generally, makes his living, and gains his political influence, through reliance upon appeal to the kind of underlying sexual perversity echoed in today's popular print and electronic mass-media of entertainment, and in the fictionalized fantasies presented in those media under the misleading rubric of "news."

This is a characteristic of degenerated cultures, such as that of the Roman Empire, or British popular culture today, in which the proposed size of the testicles of the sports arena's leading gladiators, or, such matters as the size of an actress's breasts, or the reported sexual peccadilloes of entertainment "celebrities," evoke far greater passion from the population, than those issues of policy upon which the lives of themselves and their posterity hang. As Wells expressed the same view, but from his vantage-point, "In a world where pressure on the means of subsistence was a normal condition of life, it was necessary to compensate for the removal of traditional sexual restraints, and so my advocacy of simple and easy love-making had to be supplemented by an adhesion to the propaganda of the Neo-Malthusians."

In general, whether for evil, as in the case of Wells,

_____

12. See Anton Chaitkin, "The Promise Keepers Cult and Homoerotic Brainwashing," *Executive Intelligence Review,* Nov. 14, 1997.

or for good, an idea gains currency through one or another kind of process of social ingestion. Properly, ingestion begins at the head, and is, next, transmitted from the cognitive process of one head, to replication of the same species and type of cognitive process in the head of another; but, in the lower reaches of society, types such as Wells, Dick Morris, and Richard Mellon-Scaife's circles, prefer to address the targeted populist audience's preference for fantasy, from the nether apertures of the publicist's body. In the case of the oligarchy which adopted Wells, it was his uncanny ability, like his Fabian fellow-tribesman George Bernard Shaw, to target and reach the most morally debased level of his chosen audience, whose relative successes showed the oligarchy how to shape its ideas in a form of expression which would capture what Wells recognized as the baser susceptibilities of the intended mass of dupes.

In sum: Wells did not invent sex; he merely sold it. Therein lay his talent, and the quality of his influence.

In the reports included in this issue's Strategic Study, our interest in Wells is focussed upon those features of his activity, which bear upon his crucial and continuing role in originating, beginning 1914, on the eve of World War I, a new variety of "balance of power" doctrine, premised upon chemist Frederick Soddy's assurances of the feasibility of a terrible new military power, nuclear-fission weaponry.[13]

This is the now all-too-familiar doctrine, which features the development and use of nuclear weapons as a form of terror, by means of which nations might be forced to abandon national sovereignty, and to join a new, feudalist world order, which Wells, like his crony Bertrand Russell, advocated as "world government."[14]

Within the setting of that topic, our more specific interest here, is the crucial role which the nuclear balance-of-power doctrine has had, in imposing those utopian, neo-Malthusian dogmas which have, increasingly, ruled, and ruined, and continue to menace the world's economic decision-making, during the recent thirty-odd years.

On these accounts, H.G. Wells was not only the first publicist of the argument of "nuclear balance of power;" he was also among the key figures in misshaping what became that mass youth-counterculture which, like the mythological *Circe,* took over the minds and bodies of a majority of the 1964-1972 generation of university students. As such a mere lackey, he played a key role in bringing about the process of self-destruction, which, in turn, sent the entirety of modern European civilization to its presently ongoing financial disintegration.

To understand Wells, his selection by his aristocratic patrons, and the impact which he has had upon this century, one must begin at the year 1901, the year in which President McKinley was murdered by a London-centered international terrorist organization of that time, the year in which Wells' utopian, and frankly, as he himself insisted on the term, "neo-Malthusian" rant,[15] *Anticipations*, was published.[16] This book was then a leading part of the activity which brought Thomas Huxley admirer Wells into the Fabian Society, and into

13. H.G. Wells, *The World Set Free* (London: Macmillan, 1914), dedicated to Frederick Soddy. Publicist Wells is the putative inventor of the term "atomic bomb." Notably, although Wells had publicly acknowledged this debt to Soddy in his own 1914 *The World Set Free*, no suitable reference to a matter so important appears in his own 1934 autobiography. Soddy, whose most significant apprenticeship, in study of the disintegration of radioactive elements, occurred under Ernest Rutherford at Montreal's McGill University, is among the first known, during 1908-1914, to have proposed the feasibility, and prospective power of fission weaponry. After Soddy had received his 1921 Nobel Prize in chemistry for related discoveries, his 1908 lectures, on which Wells had relied chiefly for his 1914 proposal of a nuclear balance of power, were published as a book. See, Frederick Soddy, *The Interpretation of Radium and the Structure of the Atom* (New York: G.P. Putnam & Sons, 1922).
14. Bertrand Russell, "The Atomic Bomb and the Prevention of War," *The Bulletin of the Atomic Scientists* Nos. 5 & 6, Sept. 1, 1946. See also, H.G. Wells, *The Open Conspiracy: Blueprints for a World Revo-*

lution (London: Victor Gollancz, 1928). This Wells manifesto became a blueprint for establishing the mystical, synthetic culture presently recognized by the terms "post-modernism" and "New Age." Russell signed on publicly to this utopian scheme of Wells, and never departed from that pledge thereafter. During and following World War II, institutions inside and outside the U.S. establishment inundated the U.S. academic and strategic planning arenas with New Age dogmas. These, which included Norbert Wiener's "information theory" cult, and the "systems analysis" of John von Neumann, were each and all dominated by the combined networks associated with earlier and continuing organizing on behalf of Wells' *The Open Conspiracy* manifesto. The "mind wars" psycho-social kookinesses of the 1952-1972 period of the Cold War, became, like so-called "science fiction" publishing and "sci-fi" cults, a leading playground for such queer types. Through the 1970s and beyond, the dominant figures in New Age pseudo-science, new religions, and kindred projects, were closely associated with Russell and, or Wells, like the Josiah Macy. Jr. Foundation's Gregory Bateson and his sometime spouse Margaret Mead, or, linked through the London Tavistock Clinic/Institute of Brigadier Dr. John Rawlings Rees and Dr. Eric Trist. It was through these channels of influence that that apparatus was developed for the mass-brainwashing of 1964-1972 university student populations, and others.
15. Wells, op. cit., p. 399.
16. op. cit. Wells refers pervasively to *Anticipations* as a "1900" book, rather than to the book's date of publication.

that eating-club, called the "Coefficients," where he became a kind of early-on "Josef Goebbels" for Lord Alfred Milner's imperial enterprises.[17]

On these matters, Wells' writing is characterized by a vivid recollection of what he views as the central fact of his world: that he exists in it, surrounded by celebrities whose acquaintance he wears as his literary plumage. Even world figures, including such non-British figures as Theodore Roosevelt, V.I. Lenin, Josef Stalin, Franklin Roosevelt, and so on, appear in the writing of this irascible Rumpelstiltskin as if they might be merely his predicates. Thus, in his writings, the larger world in which he is situated, is mostly out of focus, a blur. In his own mind, this British *Steppenwolf* was less in the world, than prancing pompously on stage, before it.

Nonetheless, outside the virtual reality which he describes his erotic fantasy-life to be, there existed a very real world, and a very real situation, a world in which he exerted some very real influence. That real world was chiefly hatred against the British monarchy's traditional adversary, the continued existence of Benjamin Franklin's and Abraham Lincoln's United States. This was a U.S. which he and his patrons feared, and hated, bitterly, even more than they hated the U.S.'s late-Nineteenth-Century allies, Japan, Germany, Russia, and, the France of Thiers, President Sadi Carnot, and historian-diplomat Gabriel Hanotaux. Without that essential situation dominating the world in which Wells lived, the Wells of the first half of the Twentieth Century could not have existed.

Follow lackey Sancho Panza (Wells) and aristocratic Don Quixote (Russell), from the starting-point of their journey, hatred against the United States, to their choice of weapons for our republic's destruction. There are three, interdependent, utopian working-notions thematically central to all of the 1901-1939 publicist activity of H.G. Wells, and of the Gernsback-Campbell U.S. school of radically positivist, pulp "science-fiction" which Wells inspired:[18] 1) nuclear weapons, 2) world government, and 3) masturbatory neo-Malthusianism. Find thus the bridge between the Wells of 1901-1928, and the 1964-1972 mass-brainwashing of university campus "Baby Boomers." To grasp the thrust of their "Open Conspiracy," consider that characteristic of the U.S.A. which was the focus of their fear and satanic quality of hatred.

The Abraham Lincoln Revolution

Since 1863, what the ruling British oligarchy, otherwise traditionally named "the Venetian Party," has feared, and hated, more than anything else, was the relatively awesome power which the United States's economy came to represent during the course of the years 1861-1876.[19] The facts of this history have been richly documented in books and leading papers published by this writer and his associates over more than a quarter-century. For our purposes here, the relevant essentials of that matter, as this bears upon the roles of Wells and Russell, are fairly summarized as follows.

Until the 1862-1863 interventions of Russia's Czar Alexander II, the British monarchy of Lord Palmerston and Bertrand Russell's grandfather, Lord Russell, was fully committed to destroying the United States. As British agent August Belmont underscored this fact in his own admissions, London's intent in launching its puppet, the Confederate States of America, was to force the Washington, D.C. government to accept the sovereignty of the British Confederacy puppet, thus creating the situation in which London could divide the North American continent among a Balkans-like collection of perpetually squabbling local tyrannies, this according to the same "balance of power" illogic which the dubious Zbigniew "Tweedledum" Brzezinski has proposed for Central Asia.[20]

When, despite Belmont asset McClellan's complicity, Britain's Confederacy assets failed to bring the matter quickly to the conclusion London intended, Palmerston, Russell, and Palmerston's French stooge, the Emperor Napoleon III, prepared to deploy the combined naval forces of Britain, France, and Spain against both Mexico and the U.S. blockade of the Confederate

---

17. Wells, *An Experiment in Autobiography,* pp. 643-707.
18. Consider, for example, the formula underlying the design of the scripts for the *Star Trek* TV series. High priest "Spock," ostensibly an "artificial intelligence" created by MIT's mad Marvin Minsky, represents the Campbell cult's logical positivism. "The Federation": world government. A "Prime Directive" copied from the cabbala of Neo-Malthusianism. Religiosity: pure polymorphous perversity copied from the pages of William James' *The Varieties of Religious Experience* and Sir James George Frazer's *The Golden Bough.*

---

19. On the usage of "Venetian Party," see H. Graham Lowry, *How The Nation Was Won* (Washington, D.C.: *Executive Intelligence Review,* 1987). On the 1861-1876 Carey-Lincoln development of the U.S. economy, see Anton Chaitkin, "The Land-Bridge: Henry Carey's Global Development Program," *Executive Intelligence Review,* May 2, 1997.
20. Lyndon H. LaRouche, Jr., "Tweedledum Goofs Again," *Executive Intelligence Review,* Dec. 5, 1997.

ports. When the Czar not only threatened to "make war throughout Europe," should Britain deploy naval forces against those of the United States, but dispatched two Russian naval fleets to aid the United States in the case of a British naval intervention in the Civil War, Palmerston's and Napoleon III's plan to destroy the United States, had to be scrapped in favor of other, longer-term options.

During this period, the crucial feature of Lincoln's strategy, was the rapid development of the basic economic infrastructure and agro-industrial potential of the region under his command. What Lincoln was fighting, from his side, was what Germany's great Alfred von Schlieffen defined as "annihilation warfare," in contrast to the predominantly Eighteenth-Century model of "cabinet warfare" which generals such as Lee and McClellan proposed to fight instead. Victory in battles was necessary, but not decisive by itself. Decisive was the increase of the annihilation capability which one side was developing in depth, relative to the destruction of the core-capability of the opposing forces. In the end, it was the "anvil" Grant, the "hammer" Sherman, and Sheridan, who typified the expression of Lincoln's strategic will on this account.

This mode of warfare, aimed to *annihilate* the adversary's economic-military capability for continuing to deploy effective war-fighting capabilities, had been introduced to the United States, beginning approximately 1814, from the France circles of Lazare Carnot, he France's celebrated 1792-1794 "Organizer of Victory," and from Carnot's former teacher and ally, Gaspard Monge of the *Ecole Polytechnique.* Carnot is the founder of modern warfare, a form of warfare which Carnot himself integrated with the introduction of machine-tool-design methods to the logistics and technology of war-fighting. This was adopted at the West Point of Commandant Sylvanus Thayer, whose production of a military Corps of Engineers became the germ of later U.S. military superiority, and represented an essential building-block for the Carey-Lincoln "economic miracle" of 1861-1876.

Under the guidance of economist Henry C. Carey, the 1861-1876 period saw the rapid development of the U.S. economy into not only the world's most powerful, but the most technologically advanced, by far. This resulted in the successful adoption of the Carey-Lincoln model by Japan's Meiji Restoration, and radical changes in the economic policies of Bismarck, making Germany the rising economy in Europe. Similar benefits of the U.S. revolution in industrial society, were extended to the Russia of U.S. ally Czar Alexander II, D.I. Mendeleyev, and Count Sergei Witte. The aid to Russia's technological progress came both directly from the U.S., and by way of U.S.-Russia-Germany cooperation.

Meanwhile, with the overthrow of British agent Napoleon III, France under Adolphe Thiers, Sadi Carnot, et al., had ceased to be the number-two enemy of the U.S.A., and was engaged in cooperation in the great, railway-building and related land-bridge development projects in Eurasia. Until corrupt French creatures, agents of London, arranged a capitulation to Lord Kitchener's London, in the Fashoda incident of 1898, France was effectively a partner of the great nation-building projects which Lincoln's victorious U.S.A. had inspired and was fostering in Eurasia. Until British-directed, chiefly diplomatic countermeasures of the 1894-1901 interval, the combination of the U.S.A.'s links to Japan and to the nationalist forces of China, complemented U.S. patriots' commitment to fostering Eurasia economic cooperation among France, Germany, Russia, China, and Japan.

From the success of France's Paul Barras in ousting war-hero Lazare Carnot from all positions of political power in France, until the initial successes of President Lincoln's naval blockades, during the U.S. Civil War, London was assured, that the potential strategic danger from the continued existence of the U.S.A., was a manageable threat. The developments of 1861-1876 nearly obliterated British strategic self-confidence on this account. These events demonstrated to the nations of that time, the absolute, and vast superiority of the Leibniz-Franklin-Hamilton-Carey-List American System of political-economy, over the British intellectual export to its intended victims, the "free trade" model. The spread of Henry C. Carey's American model into Japan, Germany, Russia, and nationalist China, transformed the threat to the British monarchy, from a grave potential one, into an immediate challenge to the continued existence of our republic's traditional and continuing chief foreign adversary, since 1714 to the present day.

At the close of the century, when Wells first emerged from obscurity, the American System had shown great resiliency against even the worst treason and external afflictions it had suffered until that time. The election of a patriot in the Lincoln-Carey tradition, President William McKinley, threatened to undo the treachery accomplished under Confederacy spawn Grover Cleveland; the U.S.A. led by McKinley, was an active challenge to the continued existence of the British Empire. A new Japan emperor, friendlier to Britain, presided over the first, 1894 Japan-China war, a direct break of Japan with its former U.S. ally; the 1941-1945 U.S.-Japan war was a direct outgrowth of Japan's prolonged, Twentieth-Century alliance with Britain against U.S. interests. The immediate grave danger to the British Empire was eliminated, for the ensuing two decades, by the assassination of President McKinley. King Edward VII's successful use of treasonous French officials from the ranks of France's assortments of revanchist scoundrels, enabled London to pit France and Russia against Germany, and to deploy combined French and British freemasonic agents to orchestrate the Balkan War used to detonate World War I.

Russell's expressions of hatred against the United States, like his mass-homicidal threats against darker-skinned "more prolific races,"[21] are already beyond the bounds of toleration; the man was a conscienceless beast. Yet, even Russell's anti-American rants do not approach the virulence and pervasiveness of Wells' expressed hatred against everything American. Only a low-life lackey could muster such public displays of obsessive hatred against his master's opponent as Wells does. Sometimes, as British whodunits instruct us, the household's Royal commissionaire, the butler, often a

Bertrand Russell: "When I first became politically conscious, Gladstone and Disraeli still confronted each other amid Victorian solidities, the British Empire seemed eternal, a threat to British naval supremacy was unthinkable, the country was aristocratic, rich and growing richer. . . . For an old man, with such a background, it is difficult to feel at home in a world of . . . American supremacy."

---

21. Bertrand Russell, *The Prospects of Industrial Civilization* (London: George Allen & Unwin, 1923), p. 273: "Socialism, especially international socialism, is only possible as a stable system if the population is stationary or nearly so. As low increase might be coped with by improvement in agricultural methods, but a rapid increase must in the end reduce the whole population to penury, . . . the white population of the world will soon cease to increase. The Asiatic races will be longer, and the negroes still longer, before their birth rate falls sufficiently to make their numbers stable without help of war and pestilence. . . . Until that happens, the benefits aimed at by socialism can only be partially realized, and the less prolific races will have to defend themselves against the more prolific by methods which are disgusting even if they are necessary." As cited in Carol White, *The New Dark Ages Conspiracy* (New York: New Benjamin Franklin House, 1980), pp. 74-75. The latter book by Carol White, et al., was based upon my 1978 outline of crucial features of a proposed text, debunking the mythical image of Bertrand Russell as a kindly old pacifist. This typifies extensive researches into Russell's networks, beginning my own study of his mathematical and philosophical works, during the 1950s, and the work of my associates and myself, in Europe and North America, since the early 1970s. Selections from that research have been brought to bear here, as they bear on the subject as more narrowly defined in this *EIR* Strategic Study.

fanatical British-Israelite thug, makes a readier assassin than the typical British version of *Oblomov*, the butler's Established-Church master.

After Wells' death, Russell summarized his own and Wells' common view in the following terms: ". . . bad times, you may say, are exceptional, and can be dealt with by exceptional methods. This has been more or less true during the honeymoon period of industrialism, but it will not remain true unless the increase of the population can be enormously diminished. . . . War, so far, has had no very great effect on this increase, which continued throughout each of the world wars. . . . War . . . has hitherto been disappointing in this respect . . . but perhaps bacteriological war may prove more effective. If a Black Death could spread throughout the world once in every generation, survivors could procreate freely without making the world too full. . . . The state of affairs might be somewhat unpleasant, but what of it? Really high-minded people are indifferent to happiness, especially other people's...."[22]

The distinction, and convergence of implied master (Russell) and house-servant (Wells), are compactly represented by Russell's autobiographical outburst: "As for public life, when I first became politically conscious [William E.] Gladstone[23] and [Benjamin] Disraeli[24] still confronted each other amid Victorian solidities, the British Empire seemed eternal, a threat to British naval supremacy was unthinkable, the country was aristocratic, rich and growing richer.... For an old man,[25] with such a background, it is difficult to feel at home in a world of...American supremacy."[26] Russell was speaking in the context of Britain's continuing, Churchillian hatred against that U.S. President Franklin Roosevelt who, but for his untimely death, would have quickly rid this planet of all colonial empires and also of continued British export of its pernicious, theologically, implicitly satanic,[27] "free trade" swindle to the foreign nations its intended victims.

---

22. From Carol White, op. cit., as quoted from Bertrand Russell, *The Impact of Science on Society* (New York: Simon and Schuster, 1953), pp. 102-104.

23. Former prominent British Conservative, turned leading Liberal Party figure, sometime Prime Minister, famous for his unsuccessful efforts on behalf of Irish Home Rule.

24. British novelist and arch-imperialist conservative, who served as Prime Minister briefly in 1868, and again in 1874-1880. Notorious for his role in making the widowed, batty woman from the attic, Queen Victoria, Empress of India. During Gladstone's ministry, Disraeli was the most consistently savage spokesman for the opposition.

25. Bertrand Russell, hereditary Third Earl, was born 1872, and died in 1970: hence, the reference to "old man."

26. Carol White, op. cit., p. 77.

27. The proximate origins of the British "free trade" doctrines include Bernard Mandeville's 1714 *The Fable of the Bees, or Private Vice, Public Benefits*. See H. Graham Lowry, op. cit., passim. On Mandeville's notion of "free trade" as satanic in nature, see Lyndon H. LaRouche, Jr., "Whose God Does Pat Robertson Serve?" *Executive Intelligence Review*, Nov. 14, 1997, passim. The single most significant ideological basis for both the *laissez-faire* of that heir of the feudal-reactionary *Fronde*, François Quesnay, and Quesnay's plagiarizer, Lord Shelburne's Adam Smith, is the neo-Manichean Bogomil cult, those inventors of the condom, more popularly known as "the buggers," which rooted itself in two regions of France, the mountainous regions of the southwest and along the Rhône, from Lake Geneva to the Mediterranean. The standard argument for "free trade," to the present-day representatives of the Mont Pelerin Society and the circles of Pat Robertson, Jerry Falwell, and Mark DeMoss, is a direct copy of the Bogomil argument bearing upon the signs of selection of members of the cult's "elect."

The role of 'The Venetian Party'

As previously stressed, in sundry relevant locations, since the 1439-1440 sessions of the great ecumenical Council of Florence, and since the subsequent establishment of Louis XI's France as the first modern form of nation-state republic, the central issue underlying all the important wars and related political, social, and philosophical conflicts within extended modern European civilization, has been the conflict between the notion of the equality of all persons, as made in the *cognitive* image of God, against the contrary policy of those oligarchical classes then centered in Venice's imperial role as the then-dominant maritime and financier power of the Mediterranean region and northern Europe.[28] The case of Russell, Wells, et al., is no exception to this rule. The Civil War between the United States of President Abraham Lincoln and the British puppet-state known as the Confederacy, is a perfect expression of precisely this issue.

As stressed in earlier locations, the exceptional quality of superiority of the design presented in our 1776 Declaration of Independence and 1787-1789 Federal Constitution, is a reflection of the historic circumstance, that post-League of Cambrai Europe continues, to this day, to be characteristically a corrupted form of nation-state, in which one of the two ruling classes of feudal society, a financier-oligarchy of what has been known variously, since the Seventeenth Century, as the "Venetian Party," "Anglo-Dutch" oligarchy, or, more recently, "Club of the Isles," World Wildlife Fund, etc., has usually occupied the positions of top-most authority over government and economy. Although we were polluted with spores of such an oligarchical slime-mold, with our New England opium-traffickers, our New York bankers, and our southern slave-owners, our constitutional principle was of such excellent moral superiority over that of any other nation-state established in modern times, that we have managed, thus far, to emerge, sooner or later, afresh from every protracted period of corruption by the influence of our own domestic oligarchical classes.[29]

On this account, we were not an exception to the best currents within Italy, France, Germany, and so

---

28. N.B., "Tweedledum Goofs Again."

29. This thesis, respecting the post-League of Cambrai (i.e., post A.D. 1610) Europe, is developed in numerous locations, including the "Tweedledum Goofs Again," referenced above.

forth; the highest levels were reached by such German-speaking admirers of our republican struggles as Friedrich Schiller and Ludwig van Beethoven. Indeed, those best currents from precisely those countries, provided the majority of the founding kernel of our citizenry. The difference is, that we used our distance from Europe to constitutional advantage, thus becoming the only modern European form of nation-state which gained the freedom to be founded upon a consistent moral principle. That, and only that, is our *exceptional superiority* as a form of nation-state. This is the only reason for the stubborn persistence of the British monarchy's continuing role, since 1714, of being the principal, mortal adversary of our republic. The fact, as many foolish Americans demonstrate the point, that the British oligarchy regards us with an even greater, more consistent enmity than our U.S. patriots, such as the present writer, view the British monarchy.

This is not to suggest, that Clement Prince Metternich's Habsburg monarchy was any less fervent an enemy of the United States than Bentham's, Castlereagh's, Canning's, and Palmerston's Britain. Probably, putting aside a significant number of happier exceptions, such as the Marquis de Lafayette, the Emperor Joseph II, and Beethoven's student, the Archduke Rudolf, the continental European land-owning aristocracy, taken as a class, was more aptly represented by the secret police under such Austrian Chancellors as Wenzel von Kaunitz and, the official pimp, of the 1814 (sexual) Congress of Vienna, Metternich.[30] That class, generally, was more brutish than the British. The difference is, that the landed aristocracy of the southern regions of Europe and the Americas, was a dying species, a great nuisance for the security of the United States during the first half of the Nineteenth Century, but with little potency for the longer term, even then.

As this reporter has stressed early and often, the difference between U.S. patriots in the tradition of Franklin and Lincoln, and the British ruling classes and their lackeys, is not other than, nothing less than, an uncompromisable difference respecting the concepts of God, man, and nature.[31] Russell's Hitler-like, sordid racialism, expressed in proposals for genocide, to be accomplished by aid of means which he himself acknowledged to be "disgusting" Malthusian methods, including bacteriological warfare, expresses this unbridgeable moral gulf between our respective forms of government.

To make the needed summary of our argument on this point, as short as possible, the reader is referred to the charming stories of Jonathan Swift's 1726 **Gulliver's Travels**. One must get past the misapprehension, that these are merely children's stories. They are, chiefly, political satires on the condition of the British Isles under King George I. The most relevant among these, is the tale of the fictional Lemuel Gulliver's visit to the kingdom of the Houyhnhnms, in which lordly horses' posteriors reigned over rutting humanoid creatures, called Yahoos, which latter were devoid of morals or speech:[32] an apt picture of the British Isles' aristocrats and lower classes at that time. It is relevant to emphasize here, that that is also a fair satire on the Eighteenth-Century depravity to which the British population has been returned, since the onset of those pestilences known as the Harold Wilson and Margaret Thatcher governments.

The chief practical expression of the issue which underlies the incurable hostility between all U.S. patriots and the present British oligarchy, is the interrelated issues of popular education, popular employment, and popular physical standard of household incomes. Summarily: If each man and woman is made, equally, in the image of God, by virtue of those sovereign cognitive potentials of the individual mind, by means of which man increases our species' power over nature through such means as new, validated discoveries of physical principle, then the education, employment, and conditions of family and community life of each and all persons must be ordered accordingly.

---

30. The Austro-Hungarian secret police (*Geheimpolizei*), who conducted political operations against such figures as both Wolfgang Mozart and Ludwig van Beethoven, were notoriously closer to the Venice-dominated council of princes of the Holy Roman Empire, than to the Habsburg royal household. Generally, the Chancellor was closer to that body of princes than his Emperor. Thus, the targets of political assassination under von Kaunitz tended to be the circles associated with the former Emperor, Joseph II, such as Mozart and his friends. The scandal around Anton Schindler and the conversation books, exposed the fact that Beethoven, despite his close association with the imperial family, was also targetted by the *Geheimpolizei* under Metternich. The ascription of "pimp" to Metternich, is historically precise. Metternich and his Geheimpolizei managed the Congress of Vienna chiefly in the bedrooms, where the entertainment of the distracted celebrities by assigned countesses and peasant-girls was arranged by Metternich, and the quality of entertainment provided, closely supervised and documented by the secret police.

---

31. E.g., Lyndon H. LaRouche, Jr., "What Economics Must Measure," *Executive Intelligence Review*, Nov. 28, 1997.

32. In the U.S.A. today, "Yahoo" is more readily recognized as the mating-call of that Confederate tradition cherished by Nashville, Tennessee's Agrarians.

In such a society, which our Leibnizian 1776 Declaration of Independence, and the Preamble of our 1789 Federal Constitution, define this republic of ours to be, there can be no superior social classes, nor any institution by means of which any form of usury—financier usury or slavery—is allowed as means by which one group of persons can subjugate, or otherwise loot another. Each newborn personality must be cultivated to the utmost degree possible, in the development of those powers of cognition which define each as made in the image of God. Each must be afforded, to the degree possible, the opportunities of useful employment which are consistent with such developed cognitive powers. Each household, and community within society must be afforded the opportunities which are consistent with these other requirements.

Not only must we desire this naturally lawful state of affairs for our nation itself. We can not be happy unless we are working to ensure the same rights for all humanity, for all nations.

Here, on these two points, we part company with our foremost traditional enemy, the British Venetian-style financier oligarchy and its representative instrument, the imperial monarchy.

The question is then often posed, "Can we not persuade such wretches as poor lackey H.G. Wells, that our desire is in their best interest as human individuals?" "Can the British not be brought to understand, that we wish nothing so much for them, as that they might enjoy the same preconditions of happiness we defend for our own nation?" Why not? Perhaps a miserable wretch like Bertrand Russell, belongs to the criminal class his title and outlook define his loyalties to be? But, what of the ordinary, poor Brit, or simply one of unpretentious circumstances: Why should he or she not see the wisdom of abandoning his nation's long-established policy of destroying the liberties of one's own people?

With such questions, one touches upon the existence of a principle of evil, like that which gripped the poor Confederate soldier, almost in a condition of slavery, and illiteracy, like the African-American slaves, himself. Why should he fight for the cause of his actual oppressor? How can a miserable wretch such as lackey H.G. Wells exist? Wells would recognize the answer to that question: "Eros!" Will Shakespeare's friend, Christopher Marlowe, wrote elegantly of this in his **Dr. Faustus**. John Milton's Satan, like Bertrand Russell, would rather reign in Hell, than serve in Heaven. Wells, like Adolf Hitler, another of the same pedigree, would rather be Satan's lackey in Hell, than a citizen in Heaven; on both counts, both Russell and Wells succeeded. You will not bring them back, nor, likely, any of their kind. They have been destroyed by the culture of which they are a part.

That should be warning to whose who are reluctant to give up the acquired traits of the 1964-1972 youth-counterculture.

History is so composed, that bad cultures tend to eliminate, or, at least, greatly weaken themselves. Although several thousand years were required to crush the degraded Semitic culture which grew up in Mesopotamia, when the crucial blow was finally struck, by Alexander the Great, the way was cleared for the role which Christianity began to play just over three centuries later. Archeology and related studies warn us, that it is by the weakening of a bad culture, which would otherwise be an impediment to human improvement, that mankind has progressed. Thus, if we do not willingly purge ourselves of a bad culture, one which, like that 1964-1972 youth-counterculture, has brought this civilization to the presently ongoing systemic collapse, this generation now in topmost positions of power, and its children and grandchildren, will pay the horrid price suffered by any culture, whose virtual extermination is a prerequisite to further human progress. Similarly, if we allow the British cause, as represented by Wells, Russell, and their like, to continue to dominate the course of current history, we and our posterity shall be in large degree, soon obliterated, as the levels of global population are reduced, through the "Four Horsemen of the Apocalypse," to the range of not more than the several hundred millions world population which Europe's Fifteenth Century encountered.

The central issue of all known human existence to date, and the essential issue which prompts all U.S. patriots to recognize the British oligarchical system as our republic's first, continuing, and principal mortal adversary, is this issue of establishing a form of society consistent with the inborn, cognitive potential of each and all human individuals. The issue is to eliminate all expressions of multi-tier society, in which those beneath serve as virtual human cattle to landlord or financier above.

What moves a Russell, is not the desire to exploit, as much as it is to have the status of an exploiter. What moves a Wells, or a Henry A. Kissinger, is, similarly, the passion to be a lackey, rather than live in a world where lackeys do not enjoy the privileges accompanying patronage by an oligarchy. There is, as the cases of the public sexual advocacies of both Russell and Wells attest, something Freudian, or similarly debased, in the proximate motivations of these despicable types of Englishman—and others like them. Indeed, the entirety of empiricism's history, is a history of degraded eroticism. Not merely strange sexual appetites, although those abounded; but, erotic in the more inclusive sense of placing the sense-perceptual experience of intense pleasure-pain at the highest rank of motivating passion. Exemplary, is the smell of homosexual rape in the slave's subjection by the master. It is not by our objective interests, but, by our motives, our passions, that we are ruled.[33]

Russell's referenced expostulation, ". . . it is difficult to feel at home in a world of . . . American supremacy," sums up the point adequately. The kind of republican society represented by the U.S. in its best moments, is a kind of society in which a Russell loses his desire to live. Thus, he must destroy that kind of society. It is that simple a motive. Wells wishes to be a butler to a Russell; a world without Russells, Milners, and so on, is a world which gives a Wells no pleasure, a world in which he would not care to live. He, too, must destroy that kind of society.

Thus, if we do not willingly purge ourselves of a bad culture, one which, like that 1964-1972 youth-counter-culture, has brought this civilization to the presently on-going systemic collapse, this generation now in top-most positions of power, and its children and grandchildren, will pay the horrid price suffered by any culture, whose virtual extermination is a prerequisite to further human progress.

The British oligarchy's horrid fascination with the persistence of the American Revolution, impelled that oligarchy to look at this phenomenon more deeply. Rather than simply attempting to crush the existing United States, it reckoned that it must uproot the seedling, destroy the seed, and salt the fields, such that this planet might be secured against new growth of such an undesirable plant, at last, and forever. To accomplish that, Britain must eliminate the existence of the institutions upon which the existence of modern European civilization depends. It must turn back the clock of history, accordingly. It must eliminate the nation-state, to return to a kind of global Pax Romana, or a world government approximating that. It must eradicate forms of economy which depend upon the development of the cognitive processes of the general population. It must create a world ruled by the horses' posteriors depicted by Swift's satire, a world in which the illiterate masses are kept amused, as Wells proposed,[34] and as Newt Gingrich admirer Lord William Rees-Mogg has implicitly proposed, by rutting with one another in bushes and ditches, when they are not fully occupied with menial chores of a sort which a virtual beast might accomplish.[35]

So, the one-time partners of Lincoln's legacy, France, Germany, Russia, Japan, and so on, were put against one another's throats, in World War I. Not sufficient. Some nations, among the victors, survived! Worst of all, the hated U.S.! Try again, put Hitler into power in Germany, and soon, we shall have another wonderful war on the continent! Not good enough; the victor nations still exist. Try nuclear-fission weapons; and pit the biggest victors, the U.S.A. and U.S.S.R., against one another, "With we Brits managing both sides in the middle." Stalin is a bother; as Russell said, during that period, that is a medical problem, which can be solved accordingly, that we might deal on better terms with those successors whom we think we have waiting in the wings. Russell's discussion-partner Khrushchev will cooperate. We shall bring the powers to their knees, in sheer terror of going to the brink of

33. See Helga Zepp LaRouche, "How Aesthetical Education Determines the Moral Character," *New Federalist*, Sept. 15, 1997, address to Autumn 1997 Schiller Institute conference, in Reston, Virginia. Friedrich Schiller, in motivating, in 1793, what became the philosophy of the German Classical Humanist educational reforms of his friend and follower Wilhelm von Humboldt, emphasized that the degeneration of the French Revolution of 1789 into the Jacobin Terror, reflected a moral defect in the French population. This danger, he warned, must be remedied by recognizing the vital role of Classical forms of artistic composition in the moral education of the population's passions. Thus, today, the near obliteration of Classical artistic culture from the U.S. population, and its replacement by the most debased expressions of dionysiac revels, is the major internal security threat to the continued existence of our republic.

34. Toward the end of the 1939-1940 academic year, Bertrand Earl Russell was invited to become a professor at the College of the City of New York. A woman whose daughter attended the college, brought suit against the Municipality of New York, claiming that the employment of Russell would be dangerous for her daughter's virtue. The lawyer for the plaintiff pronounced Russell's works to be "lecherous, libidinous, venerous, erotomaniac, aphrodisiac, irreverent, narrow-minded, untruthful, and bereft of moral fiber." A New York City judge found for the plaintiff, against further employment of Bertrand Earl Russell at City College.

35. See Lord William Rees-Mogg, London *Times*, Jan. 4, 1995: "It's the elite who matter; in future, Britain must concentrate on educating the top 5%, on whose success we shall all depend."

total nuclear warfare! Then, they will beg for world government. Then, we shall win.[36]

So, beginning 1964, young university students of increasingly doubtful literacy, began to imitate the rutting Yahoos of Swift's fable, in the corridors, basements, and bushes of the campuses. Some challenged then, "What about reality?" The voices from bushes retorted, "We don't go there!" One might have imagined that he heard Wells giggling from his grave: "In a world where pressure on the means of subsistence was a normal condition of life, it was necessary to compensate for the removal of traditional sexual restraints, and so my advocacy of simple and easy love-making had to be supplemented by an adhesion to the propaganda of the Neo-Malthusians."

Nuclei and Geopolitics

To understood how the images associated with the 1901-1928 writings of the lackey publicist H.G. Wells, could have become, as they did, the prevalent characteristics of belief among the university student population of the 1964-1972 interval, we must understand how modern European civilization works. In other words, we must identify the mechanisms by means of which a chiefly unsuspecting population is so subtly encumbered, even suddenly, with a new mind-set, that it is, afterward, scarcely aware of the fact, and might even deny vehemently that its mind-set has undergone an induced change to such effect. To understand that, we must discover how to discover how modern European civilization works. In other words, we are obliged to examine history in the same way we ought to study any branch of physical science.

Decades ago, the present writer, then engaged in consulting to various branches of industry, was struck by the implications of something which most relevant business managers and their consultants appeared, to him, at that time, simply to take for granted as a cruel

fact of business life. In a time when the rudiments of successful industrial society were rather widely known, one of the most interesting, and important facts respecting production, was the fact that it was possible to foresee, even years in advance, a general change in popular taste for products and product-designs. We, whose treatment of the productive processes themselves must take into account the fact of changing consumer tastes, must ask ourselves, how was it possible, that the business executives who planned the new designs of products to emerge even a specific number of years later, could effectively foresee what public tastes would be. During the writer's early adulthood, this was the characteristic problem of manufacturing garments; the distinctive feature of the rise of power of Wall Street's General Motors over the industrial philosophies of Henry Ford and Walter Chrysler, was General Motors' emulation of the New York garment center. How, for example, did we foresee, what typical women, in identified social strata, would prefer, as a style change, not only months, but even years ahead. What does this phenomenon say about the human mind, the opinion-making of those customers? What does this tell us about the manipulability of public opinion generally?

This same question bears upon the ability of the British to foresee the induced changes in cultural-paradigm which they, and their confederates brought about with the hegemonic trends among the university student populations of 1964-1972. It was not quite as simple a matter as shortening skirt-lengths almost to the hips; but, as H.G. Wells would have been greatly pleased to observe, there was a connection.

As one might recognize, from study of my writings on the function of time-reversal in physical-economic processes, this question, which I have just summarized, touches upon the most profound and important philosophical questions respecting mankind's efficient relationship to nature.[37] The question thus posed by industrial experience, is simply a reflection of a much larger domain: What *is history?* Not "history" as chronology, or chronology enhanced by mere academic commentary upon commentary, but living, real history, as history makes itself. To render comprehensible a valid representation of the connection between Wells of

36. By the early part of 1950, through his advocacy of "preventive war" against the Soviet Union and the creation of "world government," Russell states in his autobiography that ". . . I had become so respectable in the eyes of the Establishment that it was felt that I should be given the O.M. [the Order of Merit, the highest military award]. This made me very happy, for, though I daresay it would surprise many Englishmen and most of the English Establishment, I am passionately English, and I treasure an honour bestowed on me by the Head of my country. I had to go to Buckingham Palace for the official bestowal of it." Earl Russell notes that during the investiture, King George VI remarked favorably upon his cousin, Lord Portal, who was the only holder of both the Knight of the Garter and the O.M.

37. See, for example, *Executive Intelligence Review* entries: "The Essential Role of 'Time-Reversal' in Mathematical Economics," Oct. 11, 1996; "What Economics Must Measure," Nov. 28, 1997. See, also, "The Classical Principle in Art and Science," *Fidelio*, Winter 1997.

1901-1928 and the university Baby-Boomer population of 1964-1972, the following summarized considerations are indispensable.

When some among us were children and adolescents, the raw idea of history made its impact on our awareness in chiefly two ways: the living genealogy in which our own existence is situated, and the antiquity of the process of emergence and development of the language we use.[38] In the present writer's time, and for earlier generations, these two impressions converged upon one another to relatively strongest effect about the time we approached adolescence, and were exposed, in that time, to not only foreign languages, but to the importance then attached to the study of both Latin and Classical Greek. The timing of the appearance of that effect upon our young selves, had to do with our developing sense of the evolution of modern mathematics and physical science out of origins more than two thousand years earlier. The attempt to put together, in some coherent way, these three considerations: genealogy, language, and the transmission of a developing body of scientific ideas, is the rudimentary basis for a modern study of human history.

The point of this, is the urgency of freeing mankind from our species', unfortunately, commonly displayed habit, of blindly following current changes in public opinion, a habit of viewing opinions impressed upon us, in our role as victims, as unchallengeable, sacred gifts of pagan gods, of some Hegelian or Savigny *Weltgeist, Zeitgeist,* or, for the case of the most pitiable class of dupe, the populist, the *Volksgeist.*[39] Is there some

comprehensible principle of Reason, which we might observe as the underlying metric of a science of history? Is there a comprehensible ordering-principle underlying what a Socratically self-critical, well-informed mind might wish to identify as "history"?

Of course there is; that is the subject-matter to which the present writer has devoted the principal amount of his adolescent and adult life: the nature of human progress as measurable in the human species' often successful efforts at increasing power over the universe. In other words: measurable in the sense of those subjective processes of valid discovery of new principle, by means of which mankind increases our species' per-capita power over the universe. This led this writer, relatively early in adult life, to focus his life's efforts on enhancement of an admired Leibniz's discoveries in the science of physical economy. However, economy is only a facet and reflection of the more general process of practice of ideas, a practice of mankind's total relationship to the universe, a total relationship which the realities of physical economy best typify. From this vantage-point, one may identify what ought to appear to be rather obvious clues to those mechanisms, by means of which the influence of a 1901-1928 publicist might have become the prevailing ideology among a university student population of 1964-1972.

As most of the present writer's published work on physical economy and related matters, emphasizes this, mankind's relationship to the universe, and to our species itself, bears no similarity to that of any other living species. The distinctive— "ecological," if you will— relationship of man to the universe, is man's increasing power, as a species, over that universe. This power is located in the manner in which the properly developed, sovereign, innate cognitive potentials of the individual human mind, discover new, valid principles of the universe, both physical principles, and the principles which govern this remarkable subjective potential of the individual human cognitive processes themselves. In short, history is a history of orderable sequences of discovery and practice of ideas, in Plato's specific, anti-empiricist sense of *idea.*[40]

For us, as members of European culture, we must first master the history of our own culture, as from the inside. Only after we have applied the Socratic method to smoke out the hidden, usually perverse assumptions

38 . For example, the present writer's grandparents were born in the 1860s. One great-grandparent was known directly, during the writer's 1920s childhood. The most celebrated maternal ancestor, Quaker abolitionist and "Underground Railroad" station-manager Daniel Wood of Delaware County, Ohio, was a contemporary of Abraham Lincoln. It is now nearly the close of this century, and Daniel Wood was born early in the previous century. Thus, a span of nearly two centuries was represented in the dinner-table conversation of the maternal grandparents' household. This same principle is extended to the families of our acquaintances. Thus, we gain an intimation of filling some necessary place in a "simultaneity of eternity."

39.   These three, closely interrelated types of formally Romantic irrationalisms, are chiefly the donation of such neo-Aristotelian madmen as Immanuel Kant, G.W.F. Hegel, and Metternich asset, and official Prussian state philosopher Hegel's post-Vienna Congress accomplice at the university in Berlin, Karl F. Savigny. Like the axiomatically irrationalist dogma of libertarianism-cum-free trade, these Romantic ideas sprung from the pages of Kant's famous three *Critiques,* impute to history some incomprehensible principle of action, a mystical principle impervious to reason, which must be simply, blindly obeyed as "current trends in public opinion." This, of course, was the essential assumption underlying fascism generally, and Nazism in particular. It is otherwise known

today, in such locations as the University of Pennsylvania, as "political correctness."

40.   See references given in the preceding footnote.

underlying our own, naive beliefs, have we established the intellectual foundations for examining the process of history in a more general way, the competence to pass judgment upon cultures not our own, that competence which is typical of a true science, capable of judging everything. The beginning of that initial subject-matter, European civilization, is the emergence of Classical Greek culture, as typified by the passage from Homeric epics through Solon, through the great Classical tragedians, and through the foundations for modern civilization supplied by Plato and the following century or two of his Academy after him. The essence of this process of initial internal development of European civilization, is the Greek image of *Prometheus,* as that image is typified by the work of Aeschylus.

Classical Greek culture, thus viewed, is a process of freeing the Greeks from submission to the assumed power of pagan gods, a process of freeing mankind, as an idea of mankind, from any notion that the human species is anything but the noblest, most beautiful existence within all known Creation. There is a connection, of this sort, between the Odysseus of the *Odyssey* and the Prometheus of Aeschylus' *Prometheus Bound.* Aeschylus' Prometheus is prepared to endure immortal torment, for the sake of keeping secret the forecastable, self-induced doom of Zeus and his fellow-gods of Olympus, a secret which Prometheus keeps, so that the noble human species might at last be freed from the rule over their minds by those evil pagan gods.

So, as it is written in *Acts* 17:22-23, the Apostle Paul comes to the place in Athens dedicated to the "Unknown God." Paul speaks: ". . . I found an altar with this inscription: 'To The Unknown God.' Whom ye therefore ignorantly worship, him I declare unto you."[41] Thus, Jesus Christ's mission was expressed, as the establishment, in practice, for the first time in all known human existence, of a universal equality and oneness of all mankind, an equality rooted in no lesser consideration, than the fact each man and woman is made the noblest creature in the universe, because made in the *cognitive* image of God, a creature, by nature, beloved of God, to exert dominion in this universe. The Christian Apostles' takeover of the richest contributions of Classical Greek culture, as Christianity's most suitable garment for its continuing mission in this world, and the fight of Christianity against that Rome which the Apostles knew as variously "Babylon" and "Whore of Babylon," is the central feature of European civilization's unfolding history since the day the Apostle Paul stood upon the Athens hill.

However, until the Fifteenth-Century aftermath of the 1439-1440 sessions of the great ecumenical Council of Florence, there existed no form of society consistent with such a Christian principle. Over ninety percent of the population of each nation lived in the estate of human cattle, or in the debased, oligarchical status of brutish human-cattle-herders. Man in the image of God had no recognized rights under Diocletian or his followers of Byzantium or feudal western Europe. The principle which, to date, the Leibnizian Preamble of the U.S. Constitution represents with an *exceptionally* good approximation, exemplifies what the founders of the Council of Florence intended by their sponsorship of the first approximation of a Christian form of society, the France reconstructed under Louis XI.

That is to say, a form of society in which the accountability of the state for the promotion of the natural rights of all persons, as persons, was, for the first time in feudal history, placed above, and in opposition to the feudal rights of the land-owning and financier oligarchs and their lackeys. Since Louis XI lacked the power to eliminate the oligarchs, he placed himself as representative of the sovereign-state, above them, and thus, by virtue of the sovereign state's accountability for principle, made the sovereign state under his reign an efficient agency for that Christian principle, in opposition to the pagan principle intrinsic to feudal forms of society.

That is to imply the corollary point, a point which we may be certain France's Louis XI would have acknowledged as a measure of his reign's uncompleted work. The essential problem of modern European civilization, is that it has yet to free itself from the institutional heritage of what the Christian Apostles rightly named "Whore of Babylon," the Latin imperial, bureaucratic Rome of Augustus Caesar: from the pagan form of state bureaucracy. Here lies the key to the transmission of Wells' fantasies of 1901-1928 into the behavioral code of university students of the 1964-1972 period of "cultural paradigm-shift."

---

41. Compare: Lyndon H. LaRouche, Jr., "Whose God Does Pat Robertson Serve?" op. cit. Not by accident, the hill on which the Apostle chose to speak, the Areopagus, was always famously associated with the reforms of Solon, which had rescued Athens from its own self-destruction in 594 B.C., and with the Solon-Aeschylus-Plato tradition since. In Classical tragedy, Athena created the Court of Areopagus to untie the bloody knot of murder and revenge at the culmination of Aeschylus' *Oresteia* trilogy, saying, "I shall establish this law for all time" (*Eumenides*, line 484).

This, as codified by Diocletian, persisted as the evil inherent in Byzantium. This Roman imperial bureaucratization is expressed, by intent, as the permanent civil-service bureaucracy of the British Crown. It is a tradition of imperial corruption by bureaucracy, which an Anglophile spawn of the Confederacy, President Grover Cleveland, fostered, in the abused name of "reform," for the United States. It is the rot within our republican institutions, an imitation of the British permanent, civil-service bureaucracy, which has degenerated into the ruling U.S. Federal bureaucracy and judiciary of today.[42]

This continuing role of bureaucracies, and bureaucratized judiciaries, in imitation of the principle of Augustus Caesar's Roman imperial bureaucracy, is a crucial, pervasive flaw in the existing institutions of modern European civilization, world-wide. The kernel of the problem of administrative practice so ordered, is the existence of systems of rules which acknowledge no principle, but have, rather, the nature of the terms of a commercial contract, or what some terribly misguided theologians and others identify as a "covenant."

This, of course, is directly opposed to all Christian principle, as Paul's celebrated *I Corinthians 13* exemplifies the working point. The quality which identifies the person as in the image of God, is identified by Plato, and by the Apostle Paul as *agapē*. *Agapē* is expressed, in Plato, as the passion for truth and justice, as the governing cognitive principle, the informed quality of passion which guides one's cognitive processes and will for action. So it is with the Apostle Paul and the *Gospel of John*.

When a body of law is informed by this passion, we may speak of "natural law." By "natural law" we should signify the impact of an efficiently served agapic passion for man, as a sacred life of a being made in the cognitive image of God, a view of man's nature which must inform the cognitive processes of administration of society, especially those functions associated with justice. It is that conception of man, which is to be served in all legislative and other conflicts respecting positive law: "Does this decision coincide with those requirements which an agapic notion of the individual person implicitly imposes upon the society as a whole?"

This was Abraham Lincoln's conception of the law, as expressed in his Presidency, in all leading matters. No such conception is to be found in representatives of the philosophy of government among his oligarchical adversaries of that time: none among the followers of John Locke, such as the southern slave-owners; none among those New York bankers in the spirit of the Bank of Manhattan's treasonous Aaron Burr, Martin van Buren, or treasonous August Belmont; none, among the New England families of the British East India Company's opium-trafficking tradition. Lincoln's central point of concern was to ensure the existence and durability of those qualities of institution, especially of sovereign nationhood, without which human freedom, and natural human rights can not exist. This notion of essential institutions was governed by the Christian notion of natural law, of *agapē*. Among his oligarchical opponents and rivals, there was no principle, only cognitively sterile commercial contracts, mere covenants.

The characteristic of a positivist notion of "contract law," is an indifference to the existence of such principle of natural law. For the merely positive law, or the Romantic law, a stated, or at least implied, narrow putative, absolute or relative, intent, is attributed to the literal text, a text read as akin to a Babylonian commercial contract. Today, the prevailing practice, under U.S. Associate Justice Antonin Scalia, as under the Romantic school of law of the Nazis, is that what the bureaucracy, or justice chooses to perceive as contemporary trends in opinion e.g., *Volksgeist,* provides the interpretation of the text of the law, and thus becomes a depraved, erotic substitute for all principle of law. Under the sway of such combined bureaucratic and judicial travesties, there is no provision for the existence of actual rights of the individual person, under law.

It is the quibble of some misguided souls, including perhaps even most of that ignorant popular opinion which reigns, on the highest judicial benches, and elsewhere, inside the U.S.A. today, that the merely positive law is only "objectively" indifferent to the issues implied by *agapē*. Indifferent? Yes, precisely as much as the despicable William of Ockham was indifferent, as Adam Smith's empiricist employers, the British East India Company of slave- and opium-traders, were indifferent to principle, as Mandeville was indifferent to principle, as François Quesnay's *laissez-faire* expressed his Frondist's absolute hostility to morality. Is such indifference not to "close out," to "exclude," to "deny,"

---

42 . As has been noted and argued in several published locations, U.S. Associate Supreme Court Justice Antonin Scalia epitomizes, by his pattern of decisions, precisely that sort of Romantic law of Savigny, Carl Schmitt, et al., which harks back to the worst features of Rome. Cf. Lyndon H. LaRouche, Jr., "Michael Novak, Calvinist?—'Not by Marketplace Alone!,' " *Executive Intelligence Review*, July 4, 1997.

those considerations which are the victim of indifference? Can we not speak of the murderer as a person whose actions were indifferent to the principle of individual human right to life? What would we say of a man who professed, archly: "I simply do not choose to breathe"? Indifference means, in this case, exclusion, means denial, means *lawless law,* like Roman law, like the mob rule of Savigny's, Carl Schmitt's, and Nazi Justice Roland Freisler's *Volksgeist* law, like the popular law of Nero's Roman arena.

By re-establishing such a bureaucratic tradition in the administration of public affairs in the United States, we surrounded the individual citizen with denial of his, or her humanity. The positive law, and related infantilely bureaucratic rules of the game, were axiomatically blind to the essential quality of the individual person; they denied each such person his, or her most essential right, the right to be human in the sense Christianity recognizes each person's sovereign cognitive potential as that of a being made in the image of God.

In a correlated matter, by destroying the practice of those forms of Classical culture which express *agapē,* and replacing them with entertainments premised on erotic, even overtly satanic principles, we transformed many of the noblest creature in creation into those forms of degenerates we call "existentialists," degenerates in the sense of Nazi philosopher Martin Heidegger and such degraded cronies of his as Jean-Paul Sartre, Theodor Adorno, and Hannah Arendt, all moral and intellectual degenerates in the sense of Hermann Hesse's *Steppenwolf.*

For the ordinary person, caged within such bureaucratic and judical indifference to principle, what this has done, is to instruct that victim, again, and again, and again, that the principle associated with *agapē* has no efficient command over the society within whose bureaucratized rules that victim is trapped. The result of such a prolonged condition, as the U.S. population has been more or less continuously subjected to this since the untimely death of President Franklin Roosevelt, is a corrosive process, of descent into what is called "cultural pessimism." When this same corrosive process is aggravated by a reversal of a previous commitment to fostering the benefits of scientific and technological progress, as usually accompanies deep and prolonged economic depressions, such as in post-Versailles Weimar Germany, the result is an upsurge of the erotic impulse in its worst expressions, as Wells and Russell epitomize that correlation between debased rampant eroticism and cultural depravity in all other dimensions.

The U.S. veteran of World War II, returned to his, or her United States, which had accomplished economic and related miracles, in emulation of the Carey-Lincoln economic miracle of 1861-1876. By mid-1946, it seemed to that veteran, that the U.S. had resumed the Great Depression of the pre-war 1930s. The sudden introduction of the theme of a nuclear war with the Soviet Union, introduced by Bertrand Russell and his crew, as much as Winston Churchill, by mid-1946, and the explosion, that same year, of a "political witch-hunt," plunged the overwhelming majority of these veterans into deep, erotically nasty cultural pessimism. Excepting the quickening of the optimism and reawakened morality, by the veterans' generation's President John F. Kennedy, by the role of the Rev. Martin Luther King, leading into President Johnson's actions on two civil-rights bills, and the inspiring accomplishments of the 1960s space-program in progress, there was no point during the 1946-1966 interval, at which the notion of truth and justice had principled authority in government, or in customary social relations within the society in general. The 1950s flight from truth, became the generation of the "Organization Man," who could say of his marriage, as almost anything else, "Nothing personal; I'm just doing my job."

The nature and effects of this process, are illustrated by the explosion of degeneration within such diverse institutions as the Christian churches and the military officer corps, during the course of the 1960s. A summary of the clinical case for each helps to clarify the way in which Wells' 1901-1928 propaganda erupted in the university student population undergoing the 1964-1972 cultural paradigm-shift.

The 1946-1960 takeover of society by a banning of commitment to truth and justice, had a monstrous effect within those Christian churches, whose viability depends entirely upon precisely those commitments. The degree to which the churches made themselves an accomplice, in the name of "anti-communism," and the related degree to which the churches retreated from the real world into shibboleths respecting social relations in the small, emptied the churches of actually practicing Christians, during the 1950s, an opportunistic soiling of sanctity during the 1950s, with the result the pews also began to empty during the 1960s. Then, strange, new paganist cults, as "new religions," not accidentally "from below," took over the field.

The assassination of President Kennedy, followed by the folly of McGeorge Bundy's and Robert McNamara's Vietnam *Grand Guignol*, destroyed the morals of the military officer-corps much as the abandonment of *agapē* had rotted out so much of the clergy and laity from the Christian denominations. The way in which a process of détente was imposed by effects of the 1962 missile-crisis, and the disgusting hoax of military policy under McNamara at Defense, all compounded by the protracted, mass-murderous farce of post-modernist "cabinet warfare" in Indo-China, were reflected in the accelerated rates of break-up of marriages among members of the officer corps, and by the spread of deep cultural pessimism and moral corruption among the professionals. To their wives, their children, and themselves, these professionals were no longer heroes, but prospective, or even actual mercenaries.

The words often, from among these two strata, were, increasingly, "I no longer believe." They no longer believed in themselves, in even the possibility of the efficient existence of truth and justice. They had lost the passion for such things, and, thereby, lost their own souls.

In such an environment, the so-called "Baby Boomer" generation, those born during, or during the decade following the war, was conditioned during the span 1946-1962. For the overwhelming majority among those family households of that interval, neither truth nor justice existed as efficiently controlling principles of either government or private life. So, those "Baby Boomers" received the shock of, first, the 1962 Cuba missiles crisis, standing at the brink of total thermonuclear war, and, just over a year later, the assassination of President Kennedy. As a result, from 1964 onward, the morale, and morals of a generation went to Hell. The self-drugged Yahoos rutting on the university campuses of 1964-1972, warned any sensible person that our civilization had reached the outskirts of something which would pass for those doomed, Biblical cities of the Plain, Sodom and Gomorrah.

The essence of the moral and intellectual degeneration of the generation of World War II veterans and their families, during the 1946-1966 interval, was Roman-imperial-style bureaucratization of every imaginable facet of life. There were few nooks and crannies of even private life which were not invaded, and permeated by a quality of bureaucratization which one-time H.G. Wells protégé George Orwell depicted in his novel *1984*. Orwell used "1984" as a symbolic reference to 1948, when the spirit of what he described in that novel was already rampant. In that sense, the world of 1946-1960 was already pretty much a fascist world in Orwell's sense of the matter. The popular morality expressed even in the minutiae of interpersonal relations was predominantly disgusting; "hypocrisy" was the gentlest among those terms which could be honestly employed to describe the personal morality pervading life during that time. For personal life, and political reality, too, a substitute was being provided in the flourishing role of the television entertainment medium. Thus, the Eisenhower 1950s became the age of the Organization Man.

Put the same point another way. Look at this matter again, this time from the standpoint of what should have become my familiar explications of the significance of linearization in the small, with respect to the notions of entropic versus not-entropic orderings of social as well as non-living and living processes. Let us summarize the argument, and then its implication, as follows.

It has been repeatedly documented, that all generally accepted teachings of economics in textbooks, university classrooms, and correlated occasions, share in common, a single, fatal, axiomatic flaw. These teachings share in common, the delusion that we might account for the appearance of net physical-economic profit in a society considered as a whole, without considering the role of the creative cognitive processes of the mind of the individual operative in agriculture, industry, and so on. In effect, these teachings, from Adam Smith, through Karl Marx, and John von Neumann, make no functional distinction between a society whose processes employ human beings, and those which might employ monkeys.[43]

It is demonstrated, in practice, that the physical-economic profitability of modern industrial macroeconomies, must satisfy the following restriction. The argument, in summary, is as follows. A certain level of per-capita consumption, by infrastructure, by agriculture, by manufacturing, and so on, is a precondition for maintaining a constant or improved rate of per-capita physical productivity of the society as a whole. This required rate of increase of such consumption levels, corresponds to "energy of the system" of that economic process. Any gain in output, in excess of replenishing the required increased amount of energy of the system, is relative "free energy." The precondition for profit-

---

43. Cf. Lyndon H. LaRouche, Jr., "What Economics Must Measure," *Executive Intelligence Review,* Nov. 28, 1997, passim.

ability, is that the ratio of "free energy" to "energy of the system," must either increase, or not decline, despite the requirement that the per-capita value of "energy of the system" must increase.

It is shown, in these relevant locations, that the origin of what appears as the anti-entropic generation of net physical-economic profitability, lies within the capacity of the individual human mind to generate validated discoveries of new principle, and to transmit those discoveries to other minds by methods of cognitive replication. This is effected through the generation and dissemination for practice of valid discoveries of principle, discoveries which are originally generated, and replicated, within the sovereign cognitive processes of the individual mind. This social process of scientific, technological, and related progress has, as indicated in these locations, a Riemannian characteristic. This latter characteristic correlates with anti-entropy.

Thus, the sole source of sustainable physical-economic profitability of economies in their entireties is this anti-entropy, as generated by the characteristic features of cognition by individual minds.

More profoundly, it is this same cognitive anti-entropy which defines the anti-entropic relationship of the human species to the universe at large.

As indicated in those earlier locations, the characteristic emotion of this anti-entropic, cognitive process, is the passion identified as *agapē*, the same passion which Plato associates with the motive for truth and justice. This is the same quality associated with those forms of ideas unique to Classical forms of art.

The suppression of *agapē*, as by eliminating the factor of Classical art, at the same time we suppress emphasis upon scientific and technological progress, while allowing negative physical-economic decline, tends to produce a degenerative process in the morals and intellectual qualities of the affected population. The result, as Wells, in his own way, points toward this, is a form of escapism into synthetic "virtual realities," converging on erotically motivated forms of moral and intellectual degeneracy, such as so-called "rock music," or increases in membership of a Nazi party, and so on. If this cultural depression persists, the general result may be that society's temporary, or even permanent loss of the moral fitness of that society to survive.

A typical example of a morally degenerate form of culture is the world-outlook of Seventeenth-Century English empiricism, that of Ockhamite Paolo Sarpi and such of his assets as Francis Bacon, Thomas Hobbes,

and, by derivation, John Locke, Bernard Mandeville, David Hume, and Adam Smith. These cultures, are characteristically linear, thus excluding all consideration of those qualities, all non-linear, which set mankind apart from both mechanical contrivances and lower beasts. For example, in the present time, notions associated with the cults of "information theory" and "systems analysis," or positivist forms of so-called psychology and sociology, are examples of such degenerate, linearized cultural traits.

As indicated in an earlier source,[44] the very notion of "geopolitics" is an example of such linear pathologies. Generally, all of these pathologies are associated with pathological qualities of erotic states. The fact that both Russell and Wells were erotic degenerates, is no coincidence; although not all degenerates of this culturally depressed type necessarily exhibit such flagrant expressions of erotic pathologies as these two unfortunates. Each such pathology expresses a degenerate conception of God, man, and nature. By denying, or simply excluding by means of disinterest, concern for those "non-linear" (i.e., anti-entropic) qualities of individual cognition which define actual human nature, the relations among persons and nations are bestialized, as the very notion of a geopolitics, or related "balance of power" doctrine expresses such bestiality.

Curiously, it was Oscar Wilde who gave the show away, with his *The Picture of Dorian Grey*. By fostering Dorian's increasing depravity, he was self-destroyed. That was essentially what the British monarchy has done to those nations, the United States included, which threatened to overwhelm the London-centered international financier oligarchy. We were set up, and, then, through our own folly of seeking pleasure instead of happiness, we permitted London to orchestrate the 1962 shock of going to the brink of general thermonuclear war; then, out of terror, we capitulated to that shock. Our promising children, entering universities then, the children on track to assuming future positions of leadership in society, were almost destroyed. Now, we are running out of chances. Perhaps, only if the Baby Boomers themselves will face the reality of the way in which they were "brainwashed," will the new shocks of a disintegrating global financial system, prompt them to throw away the shackles they put upon their own minds, approximately thirty-odd years ago.

---

44. Lyndon H. LaRouche, Jr., "Tweedledum Goofs Again," op. cit.

EDITORIAL

Face to Face with the Unknown

Jan. 12—No one in the United States can miss the strained air of anticipation pervading these early days of 2017. One way or the other, the accustomed verities of sixteen bloody years of Bush-Obama tyranny are quickly coming to their end; all of us are face-to-face with the unknown. Surrounding this development and conditioning it, is a completely new, revolutionary situation on the entire international plane, of which the huge majority of Americans has not the slightest idea.

At the same time, as Inauguration Day approaches, some of our lower-level lackeys of the British Empire are white with fear. Will they lose some of their privileges? What will happen to them? They appear to be taking leave of their senses, as they scream out ever-wilder hoaxes against the President-Elect. Instead of this madness, they should rather be attending to "regret, repentance, and making amends," as patriot Andrew J. Bacevich wrote in a Jan. 9 article.

Meanwhile, ignored by the major media, and therefore unseen by those who read it, that majority of Americans who have had to eat dirt for sixteen years and longer, are hoping at last for a better diet.

But all of us together, without exception, are staring into the face of the unknown and unanticipated—the unexpected. And whoever is the first one to land back on his feet, ready to act effectively, will begin at a great advantage. We must be the first. It certainly won't be the pitiful lackeys of the press or the conscience-free bureaucrats who now head the "intelligence" agencies (but not for long).

And therefore no one knows what to do. How can we avoid an impending collapse of the financial system? How can we have a real economic recovery? Where do we fit in the world system? Where is humanity heading? Only those who have fought to make Lyndon LaRouche's discoveries their own, know even the first steps to answering these urgent questions.

It is for these reasons, that suddenly everyone is listening to LaRouche. They demand to understand LaRouche's Four Laws—because, who else has the answer? Without decisive input from Lyndon LaRouche, we will not be able to get out of the mess. And the lessons of yesterday's LaRouche PAC mission to Capitol Hill, go even beyond the new receptiveness to Glass-Steagall restoration and especially to LaRouche's Hamiltonian Four Laws. They go beyond that, to include the tremendous impression made there by Schiller Institute Music Director John Sigerson, with his briefing about the Jan. 7 observance at the Teardrop Memorial in Bayonne, New Jersey, in which the Schiller Institute NYC Community Chorus had participated. This represented the soul of the Manhattan Project, one of Lyndon LaRouche's more recent great contributions to the salvation of the United States and of the human race.

And you ain't seen nuttin' yet!

www.ingramcontent.com/pod-product-compliance
Lightning Source LLC
Chambersburg PA
CBHW080833310526
45788CB00020B/3523